The .Practical Internet

Includes a multimedia Book-on-CD with the entire contents of the printed book, interactive step-by-step animations, pop-up definitions, skills tests, and more!

June Jamrich Parsons

Dan Oja

COURSE
TECHNOLOGY

THOMSON LEARNING

Australia • Canada • Mexico • Singapore • Spain • United Kingdom • United States

COURSE
TECHNOLOGY
™
THOMSON LEARNING

The Practical Internet
is published by Course Technology.

Developmental Editor
Catherine Perlich

Media Specialist
Donna Schuch

Production Editor
Debbie Masi

Managing Editor
Greg Donald

Book-on-CD Development
MediaTechnics Corp.

Cover Art Designer
MaryAnn Southard

Senior Editor
Donna Gridley

Prepress Production
GEX Publishing Services

Senior Product Manager
Rachel Crapser

Text and Design Composition
MediaTechnics Corp.

▪Preface

About this book

The Practical Internet provides a state-of-the-art introduction to the Internet written in an easy-to-read style. The book includes an action-packed multimedia Book-on-CD. Each page of this innovative CD looks exactly like its corresponding page in the printed book and contains interactive elements such as pop-up definitions, interactive step-by-step tutorials, and interactive end-of-chapter material. The Book-on-CD requires no installation, so it's easy to use at home, at school, or at work.

The Practical Internet provides a focused introduction to the things you really need to know about the Internet, including browsing the Web, searching the Web, using e-mail, and transferring files. It is designed to teach you how to use the Internet effectively for practical tasks at school, at work, or at home. The first page of each chapter introduces the chapter topic and lists the chapter contents. Each chapter includes:

■ **FAQs**, or "frequently asked questions," which explain how the Internet works and demonstrate how to use key features of browser, e-mail, and compression software.

■ An **Assessment** page that contains self-test activities including two sets of QuickCheck questions and four interactive Skill Set tests. These assessment activities provide you with essential feedback that indicates how well you have mastered the material in the chapter. Data from the Skill Sets can be stored on a Tracking Disk. An instructor can consolidate data from all students, generating a variety of reports.

About the Book-on-CD

Every book includes the innovative Book-on-CD, which is loaded with the following features to enhance and reinforce learning:

Play It! buttons provide animated screen tours that demonstrate how to accomplish various tasks.

Do It! buttons launch interactive simulations that let you try your hand at the activities presented on that page.

Get It?
The Get It? section at the end of each chapter contains an auto-graded interactive review of skills.

QuickChecks
Interactive end-of-chapter QuickCheck questions provide instant feedback on the concepts that you've learned.

Pop-up Definitions & Glossary
Clickable boldface terms display pop-up definitions. A Glossary button provides easy access to all definitions from any page.

Projects
A set of projects located at the end of the book provides structured practice for the skills presented in each chapter.

■ ■ ■

iv

Use this book because...

■ **You want to learn about the Internet**. *The Practical Internet* explains how the Internet works and gives you background on the basic technical aspects of e-mail. Interactive simulations show you how to use popular e-mail and browser software. You can use the simulations even if you don't have any Internet software installed on your computer. The projects at the end of the book do, however, require access to the Internet, a browser, e-mail software, and an e-mail account.

■ **You're interested in comparing the features of popular Internet software**. *The Practical Internet* is unique in its coverage of several popular software packages all under one cover. Browser coverage includes Internet Explorer, AOL, and Netscape Navigator. E-mail coverage includes Outlook, Outlook Express, AOL Mail, and Hotmail. Coverage is also provided for WinZip. By learning how to use a variety of e-mail and browser software programs, you can develop a generalized sense about how these programs work, making it easier to quickly learn how to use new programs.

■ **You're looking for a product that teaches you how to use browser and e-mail software, but that also serves as a handy reference**. *The Practical internet* is designed to work as both a learning environment and as a quick reference. We recommend using the Book-on-CD for learning how to use browser and e-mail software. After you've mastered the basic techniques, keep the printed book near your computer as a quick reference.

■ **You're a beginning or intermediate computer user**. *The Practical Internet* is great for beginners, but it also serves as a useful quick reference or refresher for intermediate users. You can skim over the features that you already know and quickly learn how to use features that are new to you.

Teaching Tools

An **Instructor's Manual** outlines each chapter, provides valuable teaching tips, and offers solutions to the end-of-book projects.

The **Consolidation Module** enables an instructor to consolidate results from student Tracking Disks. The instructor can generate various reports from the consolidated data to show the progress of individual students or entire classes.

Check with your Course Technology sales representative or go to www.course.com to learn more about other valuable Teaching Tools.

■　■　■

Acknowledgments

The successful launch of this book was possible only because of our extraordinary "ground crews." We would like to extend our profound thanks:

To the students at Northern Michigan University, the University of the Virgin Islands, and countless other universities who have participated in classes and corresponded with us over the 25 (or so) years since we began teaching.

To our development team: Donna Schuch, Sue Oja, Fatima Nicholls, and Debbie Elam for media development and testing; Catherine Perlich for her insightful developmental editing; Chris Robbert for narrations; and Dennette Foy for developing the Projects.

To our team members' patient and supportive parents, spouses, and significant others.

To the New Perspectives team at Course Technology, who once again provided professional and enthusiastic support, guidance, and advice. Their insights and team spirit were invaluable.

To Greg Donald and Donna Gridley for their editorial support.

To Karen Shortill for her excellent work on the supplements, Jill Kirn for her prompt and efficient work as Editorial Assistant, Susanne Walker for her creative and innovative marketing strategies, Brian Raffeto for managing the acceptance testing; and Heather McKinstry and Ronnie Goldstein for their valuable QA test comments.

To Gary and the crew at GEX, Dean Fossella and Patty Stephan for their valuable input on the book design, and Debbie Masi for her careful and cheerful production proofing.

To the professors and reviewers who expressed their ideas and shared their teaching strategies with us for the Practical series: Dennis Anderson, St. Francis College; Mary Dobranski, College of Saint Mary; Mike Feiler, Merritt College; Shmuel Fink, Touro College; Dennette Foy, Edison Community College; Nancy LaChance, DeVry Institute of Technology; Janet Sheppard, Collin County Community College; Pauline Pike, Community College of Morris; Linda Reis, Garland County Community College; and Janet Sheppard, Collin County Community College.

Media Credits

∎Brief Contents

∎   ∎   ∎

Contents

.Contents

■ ■ ■

Before You Begin

You're going to enjoy using *The Practical Internet* and the accompanying Book-on-CD. It's a snap to start the Book-on-CD and use it on your computer. So don't delay—get started right away! The answers to the FAQs (frequently asked questions) in this section will help you begin.

■FAQ Will the Book-on-CD work on my computer?

The easiest way to find out if the Book-on-CD works on your computer is to try it! Just follow the steps below to start the CD. If it works, you're all set. Otherwise, check with your local technical support person. If you are technically inclined, the system requirements are listed inside the front cover of this book.

■FAQ How do I start the Book-on-CD?

The Practical Internet Book-on-CD is easy to use and requires no installation. Follow these simple steps to get started:

1. Make sure that your computer is turned on.

2. Press the button on your computer's CD-ROM drive to open the drawer-like "tray," as shown in the photo below.

3. Place the Book-on-CD into the tray with the label facing up.

4. Press the button on the CD-ROM drive to close the tray, then proceed with Step 5 on the next page.

To use the Book-on-CD, your computer must have a CD-ROM drive. If you have any questions about its operation, check the manual that was supplied with your computer or check with your local technical support person.

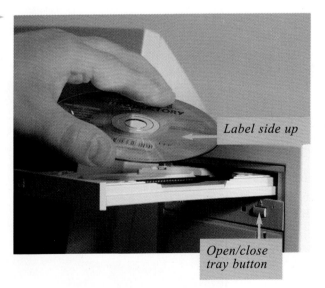

Label side up

Open/close tray button

5. Wait about 15 seconds. During this time, the light on your CD-ROM drive should flicker. Soon you should see *The Practical Internet* Welcome screen.

If the Welcome screen does not appear, try the instructions in the Manual Start figure below.

■ ■ ■

Manual Start: *Follow the instructions in this figure only if the Welcome screen did **not** appear automatically in Step 5.*

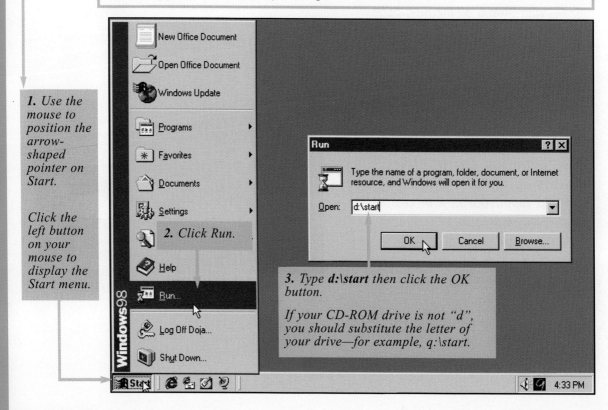

1. Use the mouse to position the arrow-shaped pointer on Start.

Click the left button on your mouse to display the Start menu.

2. Click Run.

*3. Type **d:\start** then click the OK button.*

If your CD-ROM drive is not "d", you should substitute the letter of your drive—for example, q:\start.

■ ■ ■

■FAQ What if the CD doesn't seem to start?

The Practical Internet Book-on-CD is designed to work on typically configured computers. If you have trouble using the CD, you might need to change some of the settings on your computer. The CD contains a Readme file with a series of FAQs relating to system requirements, hard disk installation options, network installations, and troubleshooting. The same information is available on the Web site, www.cciw.com/practical. Refer to either of these sources for troubleshooting tips.

■FAQ What do I do when the Welcome screen appears?

The Welcome screen is the home page for the Book-on-CD. Typically, you'll click the Chapters menu, then select the chapter that you want to read.

Other options on the Welcome screen allow you to jump directly to pages containing animations, to display your Tracking Disk data, and to turn the sound on or off.

1. Use the Chapters menu to go to any chapter in the Book-on-CD.

2. Use the Media menu to jump to pages containing Play It! or Do It! animations.

3. Use the Project Files menu to copy the files for the end-of-book projects to a floppy disk.

4. Use the Tracking Data menu to display or to print the data stored on your Tracking Disk.

5. Use the Options menu to turn the sound on or off or to select a Web browser.

Before You Begin

■FAQ How do I navigate through the Book-on-CD?

You can use either the mouse or the keyboard to navigate through the Book-on-CD.

To scroll up or down the page, press the Page Up or Page Down key or use the vertical scroll bar on the right side of the page. You'll know you've reached the bottom of a page when you see three red boxes.

If you scroll down past the end of a page, you'll move to the next page. If you scroll up past the top of a page, you'll move to the previous page. You can also use the Prev and Next buttons or press the left or right arrow keys to move to the previous or next page.

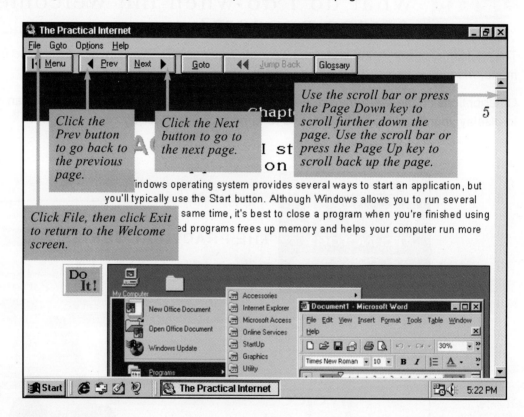

■FAQ How does the interactive Assessment page work?

Each chapter ends with an Assessment page containing interactive activities, which help you to evaluate how well you've mastered the concepts and skills covered in the chapter. If you do well on the assessments, then you'll know you're ready to move on to the next chapter. Otherwise, you might want to review the material before going on to the next chapter.

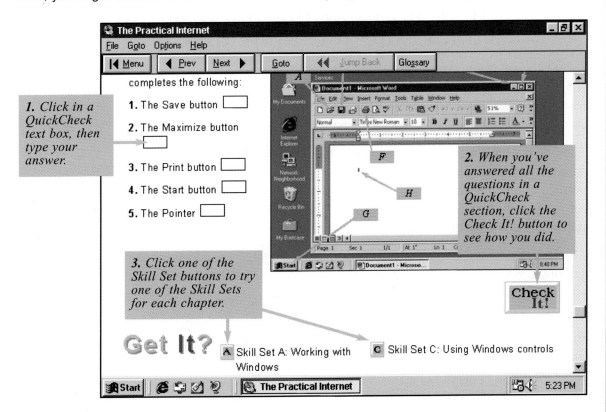

■FAQ What's a Tracking Disk?

A Tracking Disk records your progress by saving your scores on the Skill Sets. You can view or print a summary report of all your scores by using the Tracking Disk menu on the Welcome screen. In an academic setting, your instructor might request your Tracking Disk data to monitor your progress. Your instructor will indicate whether you should submit your entire Tracking Disk or send the tracking file as an e-mail attachment.

When you start a Skill Set, the program will check in drive A: for a Tracking Disk. If you want to create a Tracking Disk, insert a formatted floppy disk, then click **Create Tracking File**. You'll be prompted to enter your name, student ID, and section number, all of which which will be stored on the Tracking Disk. If you don't want to save your results, just click **Continue without a Tracking Disk**. This option allows you try a Skill Set review without saving your results.

You only need to create a Tracking Disk one time. Once you've created the Tracking Disk, just insert it into the floppy disk drive of your computer when you insert the Book-on-CD or when you are prompted to do so.

■FAQ How do I end a session?

You'll need to leave the Book-on-CD disk in the CD-ROM drive while you're using it or you will encounter an error message. Before you remove the CD from the drive, you must exit the program by clicking the File menu at the top of the Welcome screen, then clicking Exit. You can also exit by clicking the Close button in the top-right corner of the window.

■FAQ How do I get the most out of the book and the Book-on-CD?

If you have your own computer, you might want to start the CD and do your reading online. You'll then be able to click the Play It! and Do It! buttons as you come to them and click bol-face terms to see pop-up definitions. Also, you'll be able to immediately interact with the QuickCheck section at the end of each chapter.

If you do not have a computer, you should read through the chapter in the book. Later, when it is convenient, take your Book-on-CD to a computer at school, home, or work and use the Media menu at the top of the Welcome screen to quickly jump to each Play It! and Do It! activity in a chapter. After you try each skill, you can jump to the QuickCheck and Get It? sections to complete those interactive activities.

When you have completed a chapter, you might want to try the corresponding projects at the end of the book. Refer to the instructions at the beginning of the Projects section for more information on completing projects.

After you've completed *The Practical Internet* chapters, keep the book near your computer as a handy reference. When you have a question about a software task, find the appropriate page in the Table of Contents, then use the figure captions and bulleted list items to refresh your memory about the steps required.

■FAQ What about sound?

If your computer is equipped for sound, you should hear the audio during the screen tours and interactive simulations. If you don't hear anything, check the volume control on your computer by clicking the speaker icon in the lower-right corner of your screen. If you're working in a lab or office where sound would be disruptive, consider using headphones. You can also use the Options menu on the Welcome screen to turn off the sound; captions will still explain what you are seeing on the screen.

■FAQ Can I make the type appear larger on my screen?

If the type in the Book-on-CD appears small, your monitor is probably set at a high resolution. The type will appear larger if you reduce the resolution by following the instructions in the figure below. This setting is optional. You can view the Book-on-CD at most standard resolutions; however, your computer should be set to use Windows standard fonts, not large fonts.

If you would like to see larger type on the screen, you can change the Display setting for your monitor by following the numbered steps below. However, you don't have to change this setting to use the Book-on-CD.

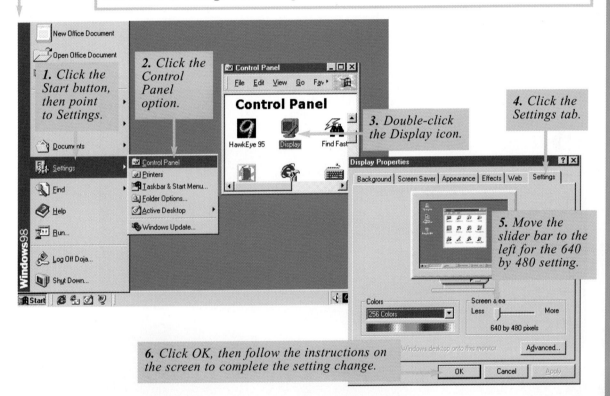

Note: You can skip steps 1 through 3 if you right-click any empty space on the Windows desktop. On the shortcut menu that pops up, select Properties to open the Display Properties dialog box, then continue with Step 4 above.

Before You Begin

■FAQ Which version of Windows do I need?

Your PC's operating system sets the standard for the way all your software looks and works. Most of today's PCs use a version of the Microsoft Windows operating system—"Windows" for short. The most recent versions of Windows are called Windows 95, Windows 98, Windows NT, Windows ME, and Windows 2000. These versions of Windows look very similar and have a common set of features that you can readily learn to use.

The Practical Internet Book-on-CD is optimized for use with Windows 95, Windows 98, Windows NT, Windows ME, and Windows 2000. It will not run acceptably on most older computers using the Windows 3.1 operating system.

If you see a screen similar to this one when you start your PC, your operating system is Windows 95, 98, ME, NT, or 2000.

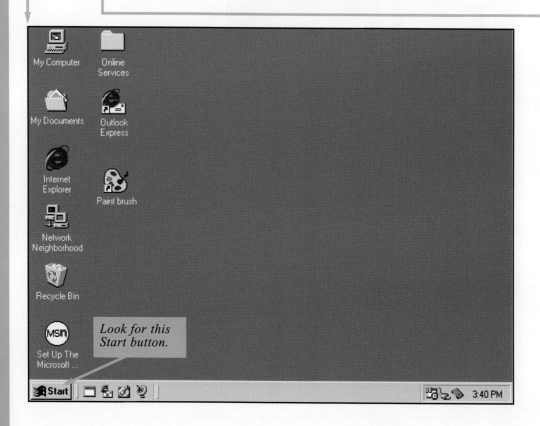

Look for this Start button.

The
.Practical
Internet

Chapter 1

Connecting to the Internet

What's Inside?

The **Internet** is a global communications network that carries all types of computer-generated data, such as documents, e-mail, pictures, videos, and music. Sometimes called a "network of networks," the Internet is composed of computers and other communications devices that are connected by telephone and other communications lines. To connect your computer to the Internet, you need three things: communications equipment, an ISP, and communications software. This chapter describes the Internet and how to connect your computer to it.

The Internet not only makes global data communications possible, but also provides a bevy of useful "services," such as the World Wide Web and e-mail. The **World Wide Web** (usually referred to simply as the "Web") provides access to all kinds of information, goods, and services. These include news, weather, sports scores, articles and tutorials on a variety of topics, online shopping, software "libraries," collections of graphics and music, stock market quotes and trading, and airline reservations. **E-mail** makes it possible to communicate quickly and inexpensively with anyone in the world who has an e-mail account. You'll learn more about the Web, e-mail, and other Internet services in later chapters of this book.

■FAQ Why would I want to use the Internet?

If you want to "know" something, if you want to communicate with someone, or if you want to buy something, the Internet typically offers a good set of resources. You just need to develop a mindset that takes you to your computer whenever you need to find information (How do I make a pie crust using butter instead of lard?), before you make an important decision (Should I take the promotion and move to Omaha?), or before you make a major purchase (Is this Ford SUV is a good buy?) You also need to develop a familiarity with your Internet tools, so that you know how to efficiently access information and other Internet services.

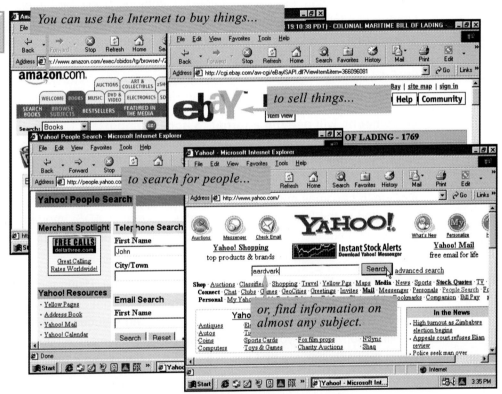

■ **Research.** The Web allows you to freely access a tremendous amount of information stored on millions of computers around the world. You can find articles on virtually any topic, locate your old high school buddies, find the cheapest flight to Vancouver, or gather information for a term paper.

■ **Communication.** Most people begin to use the Internet to send and receive e-mail, but the Internet provides additional communications capabilities in the form of chat groups, instant messaging, discussion groups, voice over IP (using the Internet's communication lines for voice calls), and videoconferencing. The Internet also offers an extensive set of resources for job and career contacts.

■ **E-commerce.** Online shopping is just the tip of the e-commerce iceberg. The Internet is revolutionizing business by directly linking consumers with retailers, and manufacturers with distributors. Online auctions are popular, not only for individuals selling collectibles, but also for manufacturers looking for such things as the best price on a truckload of soybeans.

■FAQ Is the Internet safe?

As you might expect, among the millions of businesses and individuals that offer products, services, and information on the Internet, some are unscrupulous and will try to take advantage of unwary shoppers, chat group participants, and researchers. Internet-borne viruses and online credit card fraud are regularly featured on news reports. However, with a few reasonable precautions, using the Internet can be as safe, or safer, than shopping at your local mall or eating at a local restaurant. Here's a quick look at the realities of some commonly feared Internet dangers:

■ **Someone will steal your credit card number.** While credit card fraud is possible, it is not a significant risk for most users. Capturing credit card information from the Internet is a fairly difficult task. It is far easier—and far more likely—for a waiter at a restaurant, a clerk at a convenience store, or an order-entry clerk at a mail order company to collect and illegally use your credit card number. Even if an online thief did manage to steal and misuse your credit card number, with most credit card companies, your liability is typically limited to a maximum of U.S.$50.

■ **Someone will use the Internet to access important files or financial information stored on your computer.** If you use a dial-up connection, it would be very difficult for someone to infiltrate your computer while you are online. However, if you are using an "always-on" Internet connection, such as a cable modem, it becomes much easier for someone to access your files. If you are connected to the Internet through a cable modem or ADSL modem, you should check with your technical support person to make sure that your computer is protected from infiltration.

■ **You'll catch a computer virus from the Internet.** Using the Internet and e-mail does increase the risk that your computer might catch a virus. You'll learn more about viruses in later chapters, but you can reduce your risk by installing antivirus software on your computer. You should also make a habit of not opening any e-mail attachments that you are not expecting, even if they appear to have been sent by someone that you know.

■ **Your children will access X-rated material.** This is a real issue. Children and teens find ways to access all kinds of inappropriate material, and the Internet provides yet another means for them to do so. Talk to your children about appropriate Internet use. You should consider using parental-control features or filtering software if you want to limit your children's Internet access. You might also want to periodically check your children's Internet usage to see which sites they visit. (You'll learn more about checking to see what someone has been doing on the Internet later in this book.)

■ **Your children might be lured away by sex criminals or kidnappers.** You need to keep this risk in perspective. Far more children are lured away from playgrounds, schools, and malls than over the Internet. Talk with your children about Internet safety, just as you talk to them about safety on the playground. Stress that they should never tell anyone on the Internet their name, address, or telephone number. Also stress that they should tell you immediately if anyone suggests anything strange or if they are asked for personal information.

■ ■ ■

■FAQ How does the Internet work?

You can think of the Internet as a network of interconnected communications lines that serve as a sort of highway system for transporting data. Designed as a decentralized network; no single computer controls the Internet. Even if one part of the Internet goes offline, the rest of the network will continue to function. Data is automatically directed along the most efficient route to reach its destination. If one segment of the Internet is full of data traffic or if a hardware problem is causing a slowdown, data can be rerouted.

The main routes of the Internet—analogous to the interstate highway system—are referred to as the Internet **backbone**. In addition to the backbone, the Internet encompasses an intricate collection of regional and local communications lines. Data—an e-mail message, for example—travels from one point on the Internet to another point by passing through several interchange points that are controlled by devices called **routers**. The Internet also includes computers called **servers**, which store and distribute information, such as news, weather, and stock market reports. Communication between all of the different devices on the Internet is made possible by **TCP/IP** (Transmission Control Protocol/ Internet Protocol), a standard set of rules for electronically addressing and transmitting data.

For individuals, access to the Internet "highway system" is provided by ISPs (Internet Service Providers), which are in many ways similar to telephone companies that charge a monthly fee for access to their communications equipment.

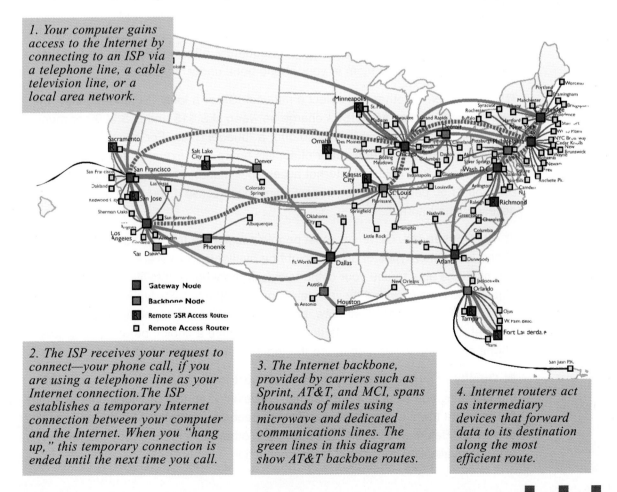

1. Your computer gains access to the Internet by connecting to an ISP via a telephone line, a cable television line, or a local area network.

■ Gateway Node
□ Backbone Node
R Remote GSR Access Router
□ Remote Access Router

2. The ISP receives your request to connect—your phone call, if you are using a telephone line as your Internet connection. The ISP establishes a temporary Internet connection between your computer and the Internet. When you "hang up," this temporary connection is ended until the next time you call.

3. The Internet backbone, provided by carriers such as Sprint, AT&T, and MCI, spans thousands of miles using microwave and dedicated communications lines. The green lines in this diagram show AT&T backbone routes.

4. Internet routers act as intermediary devices that forward data to its destination along the most efficient route.

■FAQ Which Internet Service Provider should I select?

An ISP (Internet Service Provider) supplies Internet connectivity service, typically for a monthly fee. Just as you need an account with a telephone company to get phone service, you'll need an account with an ISP to get access to the Internet. Selecting an ISP depends on a variety of factors, including: geographical coverage, rate plans, type of service, quality of service, extra services, and ease of use.

■ **Geographical coverage.** In most areas of the U.S. and Canada, you'll be able to choose from a variety of national and local ISPs. You've probably heard of national ISPs, such as America Online (AOL), Microsoft Network (MSN) and AT&T WorldNet in the U.S.; and Sympatico in Canada. These **national ISPs** provide Internet access across a wide geographical area. Some even span the borders of countries. AOL, for example, provides its subscribers with access from most of the U.S. plus many parts of Canada, Europe, and Australia. The advantage of a national ISP is that your monthly fee includes free access from any of these areas—an especially good deal for people who travel. Unfortunately, there are some towns and rural areas that are not covered by the free access plan. Subscribers or travelers in those areas must connect by dialing a long distance number and they must pay for each minute of Internet access.

Local ISPs tend to provide service to a much more limited area, typically within a city or county. If you live in a remote geographical area, you might be thankful for a local ISP that offers a free local access number. Universities and businesses sometimes act as local ISPs for students and employees—and might not even charge a monthly fee. If you don't travel frequently, a local ISP might be just the right choice—you'll find them in your phone book under "Internet."

■ **Rate Plans.** Whether you select a national ISP or a local ISP, the monthly fee is remarkably similar. Most ISPs charge between U.S.$15 and U.S.$20 per month for unlimited usage. Some ISPs also offer a "budget" plan. For a lower monthly fee, you are limited to set number of access hours. For example, for $9.99 an ISP might offer 20 free hours of Internet access per month, and additional hours will cost you $1.50 per hour. These budget plans make sense if you need only occasional access to the Internet.

■ **Type of service.** Currently, most people access the Internet using their home phone line. Other types of access might be available in your area. For example, you might be able to use your cable television hookup, a satellite dish, or special high-speed lines provided by your telephone company. ISPs typically specialize in one type of connection. Therefore, an ISP that provides telephone access to the Internet might not provide cable access. If you have a choice between, say, telephone and cable access, compare the monthly service fees and access speeds.

■ **Quality of service.** When you try to connect to the Internet through your ISP, the last thing you want is a busy signal. However, if an ISP provides only two lines for an entire town, subscribers are likely to become frustrated with the poor quality of service. Before subscribing to an ISP, ask other customers if they are happy with the availability and speed of the connection.

■ Which Internet Service provider should I select? (continued)

■ **Extra services.** At the minimum, an ISP will typically provide you with a connection to the Internet and an e-mail account. Some ISPs also offer useful extra services, such as multiple e-mail accounts so that all the members of your family can send and receive e-mail messages. Your ISP might even provide space for your personal Web page. Many ISPs supply a home page loaded with links to interesting information. It is usually the first page that you see when you log on. You can choose to use these links or venture out on your own in the sometimes chaotic and unedited world of the Internet.

Some ISPs, such as America Online, offer a host of **proprietary services** that are available only to subscribers. These special services include content channels with substantive articles on health, investing, sports, computing, and travel; activities specially designed for kids and teens; online shops that comply with high standards for security and customer satisfaction; a variety of real-time communications links to your friends; and collections of free (and virus-free) software.

AOL is an example of an ISP that provides proprietary services and content.

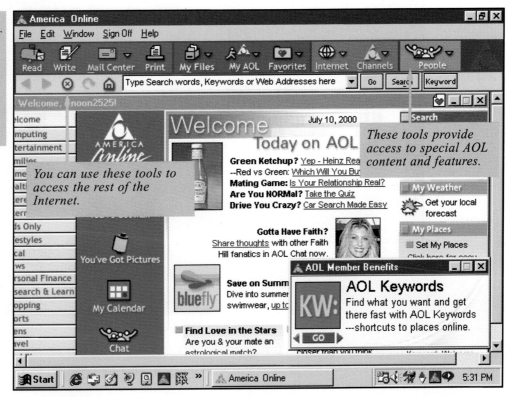

You can use these tools to access the rest of the Internet.

These tools provide access to special AOL content and features.

Proprietary extra services get mixed reviews from the people who use them. Features that are designed to protect subscribers from Internet hassles may become intrusive. Subscribers sometimes find it difficult to access the rest of the Internet or to use their choice of Internet e-mail and browser software. You may get extra features, but you might be limited to those features. To find out if proprietary features are for you, talk to some subscribers who have about the same amount of Internet experience as you have.

■ ■ ■

■ Which Internet Service provider should I select? (continued)

■ **Ease of use.** Whether you find the Internet easy to use, depends to some extent on the software that you use to make your connection, access your e-mail, and search for information. Many ISPs supply their subscribers with communications software, e-mail software, and Web browsing software. You can generally get this software on a CD from a local computer store or by mail from the ISP. Windows also supplies "starter" software for several national ISPs, as shown in the figure below.

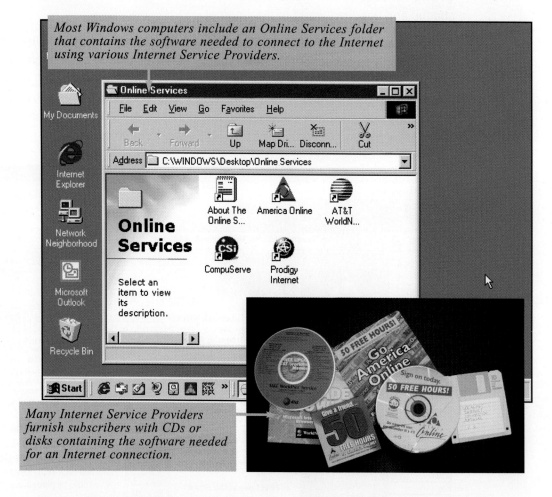

Most Windows computers include an Online Services folder that contains the software needed to connect to the Internet using various Internet Service Providers.

Many Internet Service Providers furnish subscribers with CDs or disks containing the software needed for an Internet connection.

If your ISP does not supply a collection of software, you can simply use software components that are already installed on your computer as part of Windows. You'll find the components that you need by using the Start button to locate Dial-Up Networking, and opening the Control Panel to find Internet Options and Modems.

When using communications software supplied with Windows, however, you will have to enter a series of settings, including the telephone number and Internet address for your ISP, your user ID, and your password. A technical support person at your local ISP should be able to walk you through these settings over the phone.

■FAQ What equipment do I need to connect to the Internet?

Today, most people use a telephone line and modem to connect to the Internet, so in this section you'll learn how to install the equipment necessary for this simple type of **dial-up connection**. In a later section of the chapter, you'll learn about some alternative communications links, such as cable modems, local area networks, and ADSL service.

Telephone lines were originally designed to carry voice signals, not computer data. A **dial-up modem** is a device that converts signals from a computer into signals that can travel over a standard telephone line. Your computer needs a dial-up modem if you are using telephone lines as your communications link to the Internet. Dial-up modems are available in three basic models: an **external modem** that sits outside of the computer, an **internal modem** that is installed inside the computer case, and a **PC Card modem** (sometimes referred to as a PCMCIA card modem) that slides into a special slot located on the side of a notebook computer.

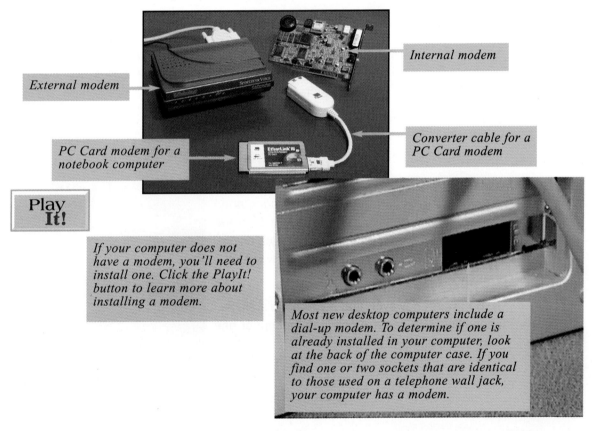

Internal modem

External modem

Converter cable for a PC Card modem

PC Card modem for a notebook computer

Play It!

If your computer does not have a modem, you'll need to install one. Click the PlayIt! button to learn more about installing a modem.

Most new desktop computers include a dial-up modem. To determine if one is already installed in your computer, look at the back of the computer case. If you find one or two sockets that are identical to those used on a telephone wall jack, your computer has a modem.

■ Most experts recommend that you purchase the fastest modem available. Modem speed is measured in **Kbps** (kilobits per second). A kilobit is 1,000 bits, so a 56 Kbps modem is designed to have a maximum transmission speed of 56,000 bits per second. Most of today's dial-up modems use the **V.90 standard**, rated for a maximum speed of 56 Kbps. The actual speed will vary, however, depending on the condition of the telephone lines between your house and your ISP. Even with a 56 Kbps modem, your actual data transfer rate—sometimes called the "connection speed"—will typically be somewhere between 24 Kbps and 48 Kbps.

■ ■ ■

■ What equipment do I need to connect to the Internet? (continued)

Once a modem is installed, it needs to be connected to a phone line. Plug one end of a standard telephone cable into the telephone jack in the wall. Plug the other end of the cable into the "Line" jack on your modem. Your modem typically also has a "Tel" jack that you can use to connect a telephone, if you would like one next to your computer.

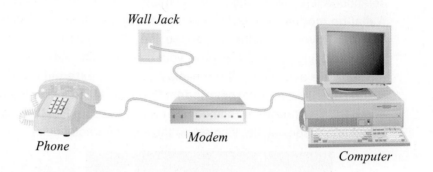

Wall Jack

Phone   *Modem*

Computer

To discover whether your modem is correctly connected to your telephone line, you'll need to "dial-in" to the Internet. For details, refer to the FAQ "How do I dial-up the Internet?" later in this chapter.

■ If your modem has two jacks and you can't tell which one is the "Line" and which one is the "Tel," you can connect the line from the wall jack to either one, then try to dial in. If Windows displays an error message, try the other jack.

■ After your basic modem connection is working, you can "get creative" with your phone and modem cabling. You can connect more than one telephone or modem to a single wall jack using a standard splitter cable like the one shown at the right.

■ Be aware, however, that if you have a single phone line, you can use only one modem or one phone at a time.

■FAQ How do I dial up the Internet?

When your computer uses a telephone line as its communications link to the Internet, it literally uses the modem to dial a telephone number provided by your ISP. Communications equipment at your ISP answers the call and essentially "patches you through" to the Internet. The communications software supplied by your ISP, typically configures your computer to automatically dial the ISP whenever you start an Internet program such as a browser or your e-mail program.

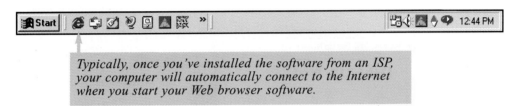

Typically, once you've installed the software from an ISP, your computer will automatically connect to the Internet when you start your Web browser software.

You can also dial your ISP manually, using the Dial-Up Networking program supplied by Windows. Manual dialing is particularly useful if you use a national ISP and travel frequently. Although your automatic dial-up connection is configured with the access number for your home town, when traveling to Cleveland, for example, you can use Dial-Up Networking to connect using your ISP's Cleveland telephone number.

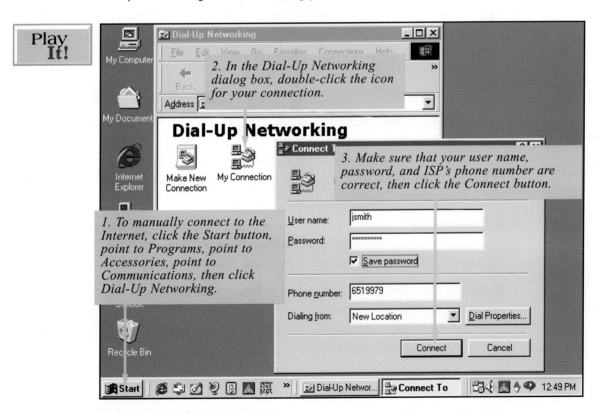

■ If your computer automatically establishes a connection when you start your browser or e-mail program, it can also be configured to hang up and close the connection when you close your browser or e-mail program.

■ If you manually establish a dial-up connection, you'll typically need to close the connection yourself. Right-click the 🖳 Dial-Up Connection icon on the right side of the taskbar, then click Disconnect.

■ How do I dial up the Internet? (continued)

The Dial-Up Networking dialog box contains one icon for each dial-up connection. You can use the Dial-Up Networking wizard to easily create additional dial-up connections.

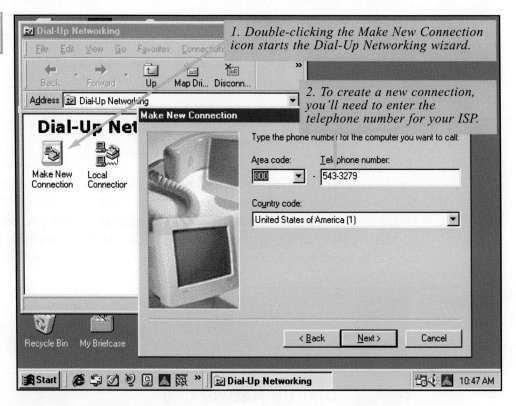

1. *Double-clicking the Make New Connection icon starts the Dial-Up Networking wizard.*

2. *To create a new connection, you'll need to enter the telephone number for your ISP.*

■ To open the Dial-Up Networking dialog box, click the Start button, point to Programs, point to Accessories, point to Communications, then click the Dial-Up Networking option.

■ If you frequently use the Dial-Up Networking dialog box, you can create a Dial-Up Networking "shortcut" icon on your Windows desktop. To do so, simply drag the Dial-Up Networking option from the Start menu onto the desktop.

■ Dial-up Networking has a tendency to forget your password. You might want to keep your user ID and password handy so that you can re-enter it when necessary. When traveling with a notebook computer, you might store this information in a file so that you can easily access it.

■ If you use a local ISP from home, but a national ISP when you travel, you might need to reconfigure your e-mail program each time that you switch ISPs. Most ISPs will not send your outgoing mail unless your e-mail software is configured with your user ID and password for that particular ISP. Check with your technical support person if you need help configuring your e-mail program for a different ISP.

■FAQ What about cable modems and other fast Internet connections?

While most people currently connect to the Internet through dial-up connections, an increasing number of people are able to use alternative high-speed connections, such as ISDN, cable modems, direct satellite service (DSS), or ADSL. Whereas a dial-up connection typically has a maximum transfer rate of 56 Kbps, some high-speed connections offer speeds that are measured, not in thousands of bits per second (Kbps), but in millions of bits per second (Mbps).

High speed connections mean fast data transfer rates, which translate to quick action when working on the Web. For example, video clips and sound files that are choppy when transferred over a dial-up connection play smoothly when they arrive at your computer over a high-speed connection.

High-speed connections offer many advantages, but may increase the risk that an unauthorized person will access your computer system. Most high-speed connections are **always-on connections**—your computer is, in effect, always connected to your ISP so that you don't have to wait for for the completion of a dialing sequence each time that you use the Internet. Always-on cable modems and ADSL services use local area network technology to connect customers to the ISP's communications equipment. Under some circumstances, the cable that connects you to the ISP, can also be used by other customers to gain unauthorized access to your computer. If you are considering cable modem or ADSL service, make sure that your ISP provides security measures that prevent intrusion from unauthorized access.

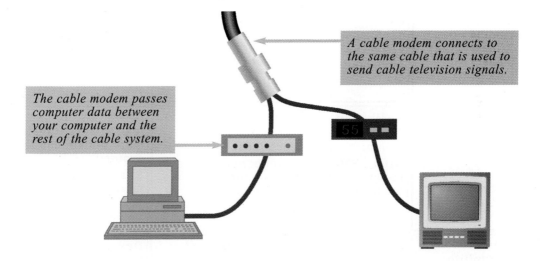

A cable modem connects to the same cable that is used to send cable television signals.

The cable modem passes computer data between your computer and the rest of the cable system.

Unfortunately, high-speed connections are not available in all areas. You'll need to check with local suppliers to see which, if any, high-speed connections are available where you live. Your telephone book is a good source of information about high-speed Internet access in your local area. Check under the listings for "Internet." You can contact your cable television company and ask if it provides Internet service. For ISDN and ADSL availability check with your telephone company or local communication companies.

■ What about cable modems and other fast Internet connections? (continued)

To select the type of high-speed connection that's right for you, you'll need to consider a number of factors, such as speed, setup costs, monthly fees, and security. The table below provides some general comparative information. For specific details, you should contact high-speed access providers in your area.

Internet Connection Options			
	Speed & Cost	**Advantages**	**Disadvantages**
Dial-up Uses a standard telephone line	28.8 - 56 Kbps; Minimal cost; No setup fee	Available everywhere; Inexpensive—if you use your existing telephone line, you have only to pay the monthly ISP fee	Slowest transfer speed; Takes a long time to dial-up each time you access the Internet; When many subscribers are trying to connect, you might get a busy signal
ISDN Uses a specially conditioned telephone line	64 Kbps or 128 Kbps; $20 - $50 per month; Up to $500 setup fee	Available in many locations; Dial-up connection is established almost instantly	Relatively expensive, compared to faster options such as ADSL and Cable Modems
ADSL Uses a specially conditioned telephone line and special modem	700 Kbps - 1.5 Mbps; $40 - $200 per month; $500 - $1,000 setup fee and equipment cost	Very fast connection; Not shared with any other users, so performance will not degrade as more users are added to the service; Connection time is instantaneous	Data going to the Internet may be limited to lower speeds than data coming from the Internet; Always-on connection can make your computer more susceptible to Internet hackers
Cable Modem Uses a special modem connected to your cable TV line	2 -10 Mbps; $30 - $60 per month; $100 - $200 setup fee and equipment cost	Very fast connection; Available in many locations; Connection time is instantaneous	Shared use of cable can lead to slow transfers as more people use the system; Shared use of the cable increases the chances that someone else on that cable can access your computer
Direct Satellite Service Uses a satellite dish for data coming to your computer	400 Kbps; $30 - $100 per month; $300 - $800 setup fee and satellite cost	Available in most locations; High-speed downloads work well for Web browsing; Requires an external satellite dish	Data going to the Internet is typically sent using a standard modem and is limited to 56 Kbps; May require a dial-up ISP in addition to satellite service

■   ■   ■

QuickCheck

1. The main routes of the Internet—analogous to the interstate highway system—are referred to as the Internet _____.

2. Most computers use a modem to establish a dial-up connection to a(n) _____.

3. Some ISPs provide _____ extra features—content and services available only to subscribers.

4. True or false? After you install the communications software from an ISP, your computer will typically dial up and connect to the Internet whenever you start an Internet program such as a browser. _____

5. Computers of many different types are able to communicate with each other over the Internet because of a set of standard rules, or protocol, called _____.

Check It!

QuickCheck B

Match the lettered definitions on the right with the terms on the left:

1. ISDN _____

2. Cable Modem service _____

3. ADSL _____

4. Dial-up _____

5. DSS _____

a. Uses a standard phone line and dial-up modem to create a connection typically between 28.8 and 56 Kbps.

b. An "always-on" connection that uses a specially conditioned telephone line and modem to access the Internet.

c. A specially conditioned phone line that makes an almost instantaneous connection every time that you access the Internet.

d. An Internet connection that uses a satellite dish to receive data from the Internet, but uses a dial-up ISP to send data to the Internet.

e. An Internet access service provided by a cable television company.

Check It!

Get It?   A Skill Set A: Connecting to the Internet

Chapter 2

Browser Basics

What's Inside?

The real action on the Internet takes place on the Web, an Internet service that was introduced in 1989. Every day, millions of people access Web pages that contain information, provide shopping opportunities, offer free software and music, supply the local weather forecast, and provide a host of other services. A **Web page** is a specially coded document that can contain text, graphics, videos, and sounds. These pages are stored on Web servers all over the world. A **Web server** is a computer, attached to the Internet, that runs special Web server software and that can send Web pages out to other computers via the Internet. A **Web site** consists of one or more Web pages located on a Web server. Each Web page is assigned a **URL** (Universal Resource Locator) that uniquely identifies its location on the Internet.

A **Web browser**—usually simply referred to as a "browser"—is a program that runs on your computer and helps you to access Web pages. Currently, the three most popular browsers are Microsoft Internet Explorer, Netscape Navigator, and the AOL browser. This chapter presents the basic techniques that you'll need for using any of these browsers.

■FAQ How do I start my browser?

No matter which browser you're using, you'll probably start it by clicking an icon on the Windows taskbar. As an alternative, you can also click the Start button, then locate your browser on the Programs menu. Your browser is typically configured to automatically connect your computer to the Internet. If not, you can use Dial-Up Networking to connect manually. (See the Chapter 1 FAQ "How do I dial up the Internet?")

When you start a browser, it automatically loads and displays a page from a Web site. This starting page is known as your **home page**. Scroll bars allow you to scroll vertically and horizontally over pages that are too large to fit in the current window. Your browser window contains a menu bar and a toolbar that provide access to commands, configuration settings, and online help. Your browser window also includes an **Address box** into which you can type a URL. A status bar, located at the bottom of your browser window, keeps you updated on the status of Web pages as they arrive at your computer.

Internet Explorer is the most popular Web browser. It is included with most versions of Windows, so it is probably already installed on your computer. To start Internet Explorer, click the icon, located on the Windows taskbar at the bottom of your computer screen.

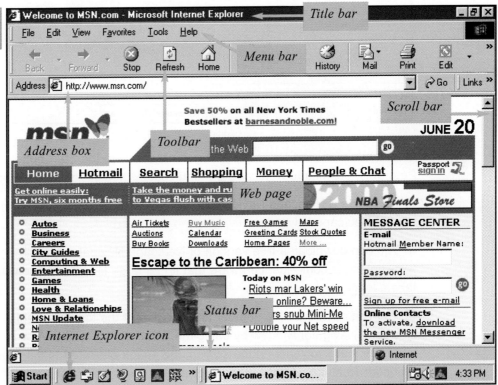

■ You can also start Internet Explorer by clicking Start, pointing to Programs, then clicking Internet Explorer.

■ If you see an Internet Explorer icon on your Windows desktop, you can double-click it to start Internet Explorer.

■ How do I start my browser? (continued)

Netscape Navigator was one of the first commercially available browsers, and it remains popular today. If it has been installed on your computer, you'll typically find the Netscape Navigator icon on the Windows taskbar at the bottom of your screen. Clicking this icon is the easiest way to start the Netscape Navigator browser.

NETSCAPE
NAVIGATOR

■ You can also start Netscape Navigator by clicking the Start button, pointing to Programs, pointing to Netscape Communicator, then clicking Netscape Navigator.

■ If you see a Netscape Navigator icon on your desktop, you can double-click it to start Netscape Navigator.

■ You can download a free version of Netscape Navigator from www.netscape.com—just be aware that it is a large file and the download might take a long time.

■ You can customize the number and position of the toolbars displayed in the Netscape Navigator window by using the Show option on the View menu. When you have many toolbars on the screen, the space allocated to the Web page is reduced. To make a larger window for a Web page, you might want to remove the toolbar that contains the Instant Message and WebMail buttons.

■ How do I start my browser? (continued)

The **AOL browser** is proprietary software supplied only to AOL subscribers. To start AOL, click the ▲ AOL icon on the Windows taskbar, located at the bottom of your computer screen. When you go online with AOL, the main screen includes a browser toolbar with buttons and an Address box. You don't have to take any additional steps to start the browser.

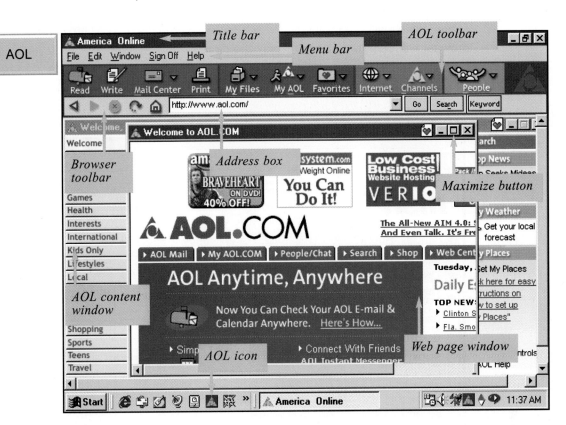

■ You can also start AOL by clicking the Start button, then clicking America Online at the top of the Start menu.

■ If you see an AOL icon on your desktop, you can double-click it to start AOL.

■ If Web pages appear in a separate window, click the ▫ Maximize button to integrate the Web page window with the larger AOL window.

■ The AOL browser is actually a modified version of Internet Explorer. You'll see the similarity later in the chapter when you use both browsers to change your home page.

■FAQ How do I use a URL to go to a Web site?

A **URL** (Universal Resource Locator) serves as an address to uniquely identify a Web page. You'll see URLs on everything from billboard ads, to soup cans and business cards. To enter a URL, first click the Address box on the Internet Explorer, Netscape Navigator, or AOL browser window. Next, type the URL, then press the Enter key. Your browser will send a request for this URL to the Web server, which will then transmit the requested Web page to your browser. Your browser will then format and display the page on your computer screen.

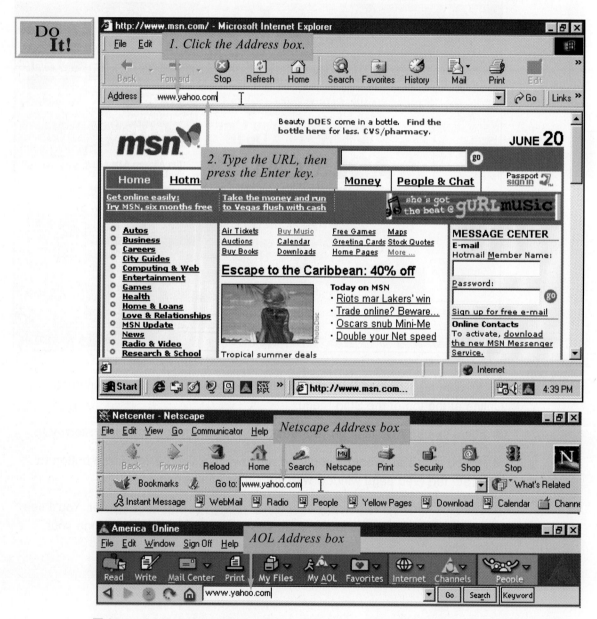

■ You must be very precise when entering a URL. Don't use any spaces—even before or after punctuation marks—and make sure that you use the exact mix of uppercase and lowercase letters.

■ A complete URL usually starts with http:// as in http://www.ibm.com. However, you usually don't need to type the http:// part of the URL.

■FAQ How do I use links on a Web page?

A **link** is a connection, or path, between two Web pages. It contains the URL of a Web page, and so it can be used to "jump" from one Web page to another. Links are usually displayed on a Web page as underlined text or as a graphic. When positioned over a link, the arrow-shaped pointer turns into a 🖑. When you click a link, the requested Web page will be transmitted from the Web server and displayed on your computer.

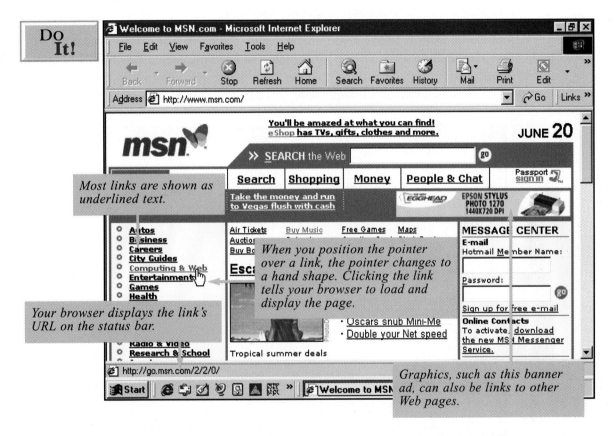

Do It!

Most links are shown as underlined text.

Your browser displays the link's URL on the status bar.

When you position the pointer over a link, the pointer changes to a hand shape. Clicking the link tells your browser to load and display the page.

Graphics, such as this banner ad, can also be links to other Web pages.

■ Text links often change color after you click them. The color change makes it easy for you to see which links you have already clicked and viewed.

■ To discover if a graphic is a link, move the pointer over the graphic. If the pointer changes to a hand shape, then the graphic is linked to another Web page or media element.

■ If your browser is configured to display a status bar, when you move the pointer over a link, the link's URL will be displayed in the status bar. For example, in the figure above, the hand is pointing to the Computing & Web link. On the status bar, you can see that the URL for this link is http://go.msn/2/2/0/. By being aware of what's shown in the status bar, you can get an idea of a link's destination before you click it.

■FAQ What's the purpose of the Stop and Home buttons?

Usually, when you click a link or enter a URL, a Web page appears fairly quickly. The "load time" from when you request a page until it is displayed should only be a matter of seconds. Sometimes, however, a Web page might load very slowly or not appear to load at all. If you don't want to wait for a page to load, click the **Stop button** on the toolbar. The loading process will stop, typically without displaying the Web page, but sometimes just a partial page Web page will be displayed. You can then click a different link or enter a new URL.

The **Home button** displays your home page—the page that is displayed when you first start your browser. Clicking this button at any time during an Internet session returns you to your home page. Later in this chapter, you'll learn how to set your home page to a Web site that provides you with lots of links to useful information.

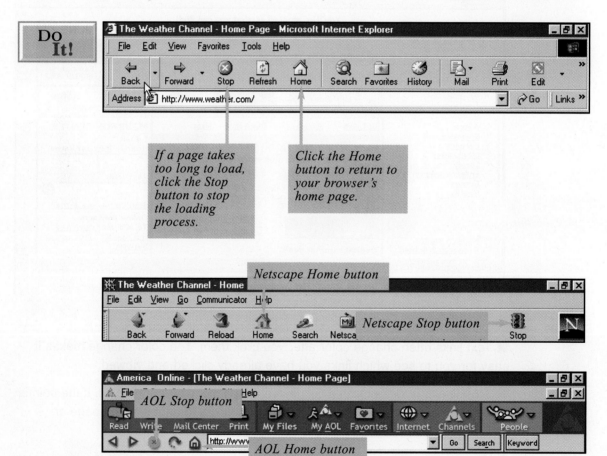

If a page takes too long to load, click the Stop button to stop the loading process.

Click the Home button to return to your browser's home page.

Netscape Home button

Netscape Stop button

AOL Stop button

AOL Home button

■ If a page seems to load very slowly, click the Stop button, then click the link again. Sometimes the page will load much faster on the second attempt. If the page still won't load, try a different link or enter a different URL.

■ The **Refresh button** tells your browser to reload the current page. You won't use this button very often, but sometimes if you use the Stop button, then click the Refresh button, the page might reload correctly.

■FAQ How do the Back and Forward buttons work?

The **Back button** displays the last page that you viewed. You can click this button several times to step back through a series of pages that you've previously viewed.

Contrary to what you might expect, the **Forward button** does not take you to new pages that you haven't yet viewed. Instead the Forward button essentially counteracts the Back button. If you click the Back button to go back to a page, you can then click the Forward button to return to the page that you were viewing before you clicked the Back button.

When you first start your browser, the Back and Forward buttons will be disabled or "grayed out." The Back button will become enabled when you go to a new page. The Forward button will become enabled after you use the Back button to go back to a previously viewed page.

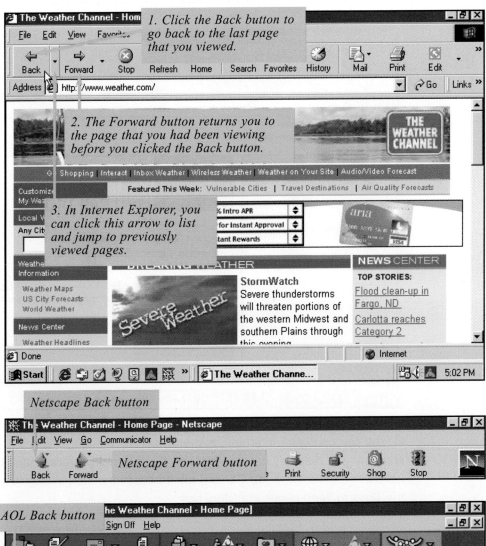

1. Click the Back button to go back to the last page that you viewed.

2. The Forward button returns you to the page that you had been viewing before you clicked the Back button.

3. In Internet Explorer, you can click this arrow to list and jump to previously viewed pages.

Netscape Back button

Netscape Forward button

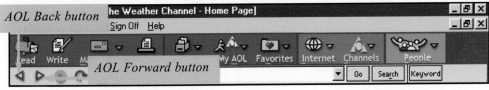

AOL Back button

AOL Forward button

■FAQ How does the History list work?

The Back button and the Forward button make it easy for you to jump back to Web pages that you recently visited. However, the Back and Forward buttons only keep track of pages that you've visited in the current session. They won't help you to locate pages that you visited yesterday or the day before that. To help you access these sites again, your browser provides a History list and a site list.

A **History list** displays the titles and/or URLs of individual Web *pages* that you visited in the past. A similar list, called the **site list**, displays the URLs of previously visited Web *sites*. For example, whereas the History list might include the URL for a Home Depot page about cabinets—www.homedepot.com/kitchens/cabinets.html— the site list will include the URL for Home Depot's main page—www.homedepot.com.

To access Internet Explorer's History list, click the History button on the toolbar. To access the site list, click the down-arrow button on the right side of the Address box.

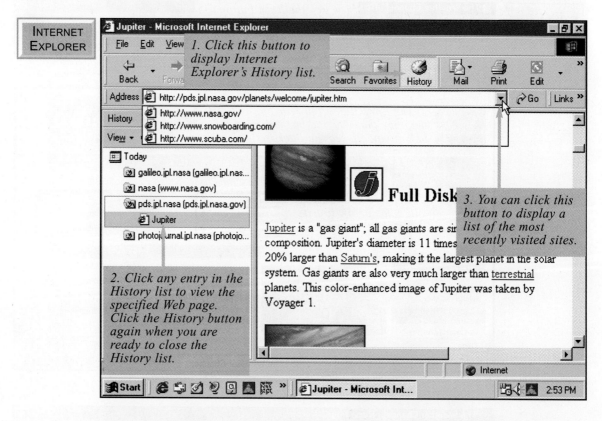

■ You can configure Internet Explorer to set the number of days that it retains entries in the History list. Click Tools on the Internet Explorer menu bar, then click Internet Options. Click the General tab if necessary, then change the number in the *Days to keep pages in history* box.

■ **How does the History list work? (continued)**

Netscape Navigator's History list appears in a separate window and contains a list of Web pages that you've previously visited. The History list is accessible from the Communicator menu. A site list is also available. Simply click the down-arrow button on the right side of the Address box.

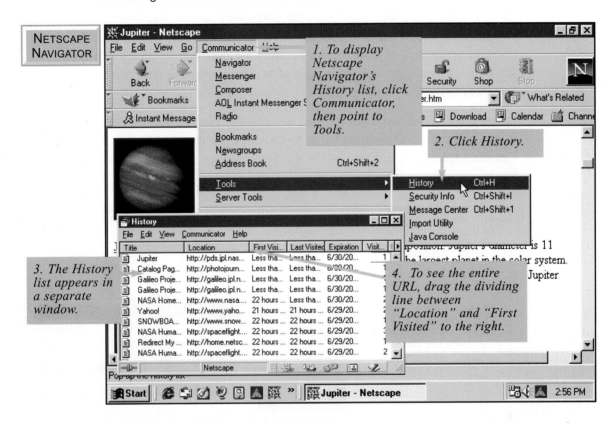

AOL doesn't include a full History list feature. However, you can click the down-arrow button on the right side of the AOL Address box to display the titles of recently viewed Web pages.

■ Remember that the History list retains a record of every Web page that you have visited. Anyone with access to your computer can check the History list to see this list. If you don't want anyone else to see the pages that you have visited, you can clear the History list as explained in the next chapter.

■FAQ How can I use Favorites or Bookmarks to go back to useful sites?

As you continue to use the Web, you'll realize that you visit some pages on a regular basis. For example, you might regularly visit www.weather.com to check your local weather forecast. Rather than typing the URL every time you want to visit a particular Web page, you can add it to your list of **Favorites** (as they are called in Internet Explorer and AOL), or **Bookmarks** (as they are called in Netscape Navigator). After you've added a page to your list of favorites, you can then just open the Favorites list and click the page that you want to view.

When you use Internet Explorer, you can use the Favorites button on the toolbar to add pages to the Favorites list or to select pages that you want to view. The Favorites list appears in a separate window. To close this window, click the Favorites button again.

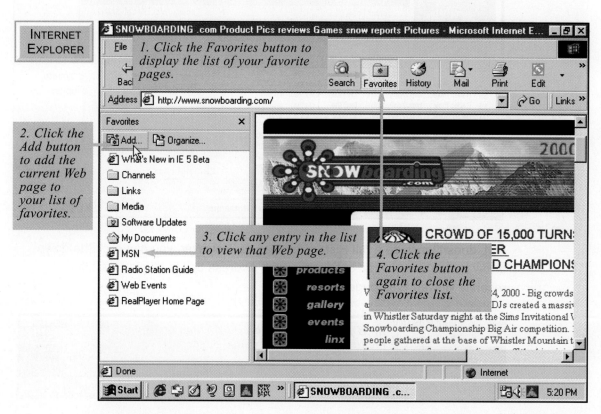

INTERNET EXPLORER

1. Click the Favorites button to display the list of your favorite pages.

2. Click the Add button to add the current Web page to your list of favorites.

3. Click any entry in the list to view that Web page.

4. Click the Favorites button again to close the Favorites list.

■ You can also use a menu to access the Favorites list. To add the current page to the list, click Favorites on the Internet Explorer menu bar, then click Add to Favorites. To visit a site on the Favorites list, click Favorites, then click the site that you want to visit.

■ You can group your favorite Web pages into folders using the Organize button, located at the top of the Favorites list.

■ To delete a Favorite site or folder, right-click it, then click Delete on the shortcut menu. Internet Explorer includes a number of predefined Favorite sites and folders. You might want to delete some of them if they don't interest you.

■ How do I use Favorites or Bookmarks to go back to useful sites? (continued)

Netscape Navigator uses the term Bookmarks, instead of Favorites, and provides a Bookmarks button on the same toolbar that contains the Address box. Use this button to display a list of bookmarked Web pages, then select the one that you want to view. When adding a Web page to the list of Bookmarks, make sure that the page is displayed in your browser window before you click the Bookmarks button.

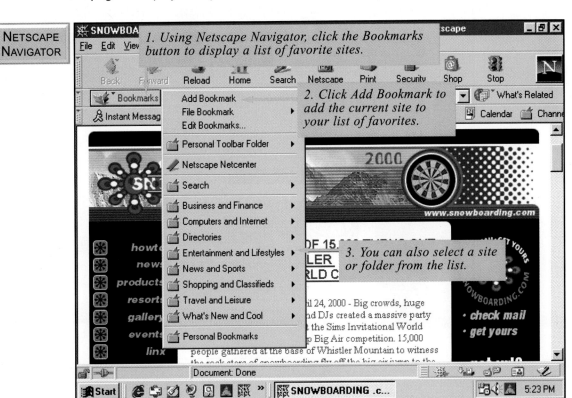

■ You can also use a menu to access your Bookmarks. Click Communicator on the Netscape Navigator menu bar, then click the Bookmark that you want to view.

■ You can organize your bookmarked Web pages into folders by using the Edit Bookmarks option from the Bookmarks menu. The Edit window contains a list of your Bookmarks and allows you to drag them from one folder to another. To create new folders for your Bookmarks, click the File menu, then click the New Folder option.

■ To delete a Bookmark, open the Bookmarks menu and click Edit Bookmarks. Right-click any Bookmark or folder that's listed in the editing window, then click Delete Bookmark on the shortcut menu.

■ Netscape Navigator includes quite a few predefined Bookmarks. You might want to delete those that don't interest you.

■ How do I use Favorites or Bookmarks to go back to useful sites? (continued)

AOL's Favorites list is easy to use. To add a site to the Favorites list, go to the site, click the Favorites button on the AOL toolbar, then click *Add Top Window to Favorite Places*. To view a Web page that's listed in Favorites, click the Favorites button, then click the name of the page.

AOL

Using AOL, click the Favorites button to display the Favorites menu.

To add a page to the Favorites list, first make sure that the page is displayed. Then click Add Top Window to Favorite Places.

To select a Web page or folder from the list, click it.

■ To delete a Web page or folder from the Favorites list, click the Favorites button on the toolbar, then click Favorite Places. Click the folder or site that you want to delete, then click the Delete button.

■ AOL includes a number of predefined Favorites in a variety of categories. You can delete them if they don't interest you.

■FAQ What should I do when I get a "Page Not Found" message?

Sometimes when you click a link or type a URL, your browser will display a "Page Not Found" message. This message appears if a Web page does not exist or if the server cannot, for some reason, send the requested Web page back to the browser.

If you haven't mistyped the URL, the "Page Not Found" message probably means that the Web site has been updated and the page has been moved, renamed, or deleted. Occasionally, the "Page Not Found" message will appear if a Web site is too busy to respond to the request from your browser. If you wait and try to access the page later, you might have better success.

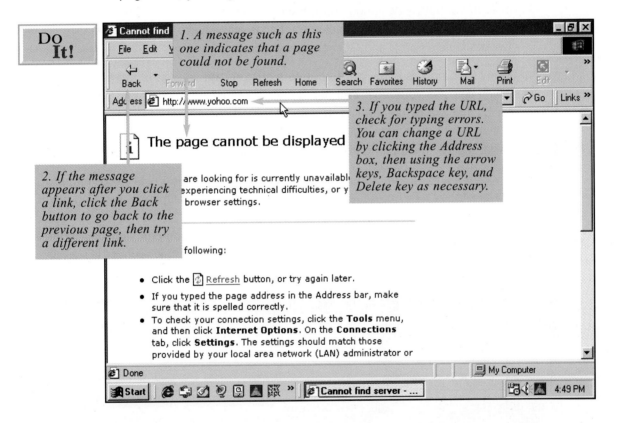

Do It!

1. A message such as this one indicates that a page could not be found.

2. If the message appears after you click a link, click the Back button to go back to the previous page, then try a different link.

3. If you typed the URL, check for typing errors. You can change a URL by clicking the Address box, then using the arrow keys, Backspace key, and Delete key as necessary.

■ Sometimes you'll click a link and a message will indicate that the page has moved to a new location. Usually, you'll automatically be redirected to the new site. If not, you'll be provided with a link to the new location of the page.

■ If you've entered a URL such as www.mtc.com/info/visitors /main.html and get a "Page Not Found" message, you might be able to use the following trick to locate the page. Click the Address box, then delete the part of the URL that appears after the last /. Press the Enter key to see if you can connect to a page using that URL. If that doesn't work, click the Address box again, delete the next part of the URL, and press the Enter key to try again. If you find a URL that works, you might then be able to follow the links from that page to locate the information that you need.

■FAQ How do I change my home page?

Each time that you start your browser or click the Home button, your browser displays the Web page that has been designated as your home page. Most browsers provide a menu option that allows you to change your home page.

Typically, you'll want to designate a Web portal as your home page. A **Web portal** is a Web page or site that contains a collection of links, services, and content designed to be useful to the typical Internet user. Most Web portals include links to news, weather, sports scores, shopping sites, and chat rooms. In addition, these sites usually provide a way to search the Web for information. Popular Web portals include Yahoo! (www.yahoo.com), Excite (www.excite.com), MSN.com (www.msn.com), AOL (www.aol.com), Lycos (www.lycos.com), AltaVista (www.altavista.com), and GO.com (www.go.com).

Many Web portals allow you to create a customized version of the portal page, which displays your local weather, quotes for stocks that you own, news stories on topics that are of interest to you, and sports scores for your favorite teams. These portals might even offer free e-mail accounts and space for your personal Web page. It's worth exploring the options to find a portal site that will work for you.

If you're using Internet Explorer as your browser, changing your home page to a portal site is easy. From the Tools menu, select Internet Options. A dialog box will provide you with an Address box for your home page URL. You can either enter a URL or, if the portal that you want to use is displayed, you can simply click the Use Current button. Your new home page will take effect as soon as you click the OK button.

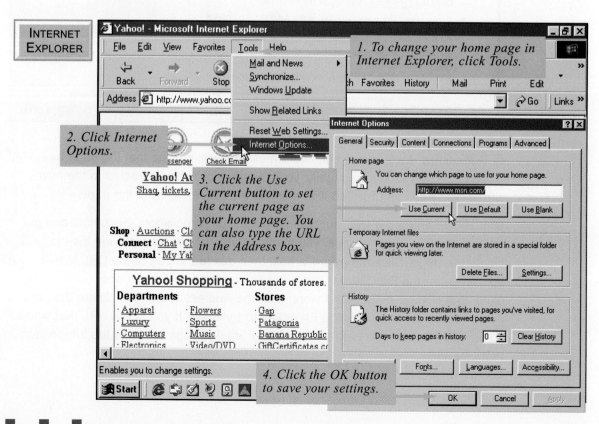

INTERNET EXPLORER

1. To change your home page in Internet Explorer, click Tools.

2. Click Internet Options.

3. Click the Use Current button to set the current page as your home page. You can also type the URL in the Address box.

4. Click the OK button to save your settings.

■ How do I change my home page? (continued)

Netscape Navigator uses http://home.netscape.com as the default home page. This page provides helpful information about the Netscape Corporation and Netscape products. However, you can easily change the home page as explained below.

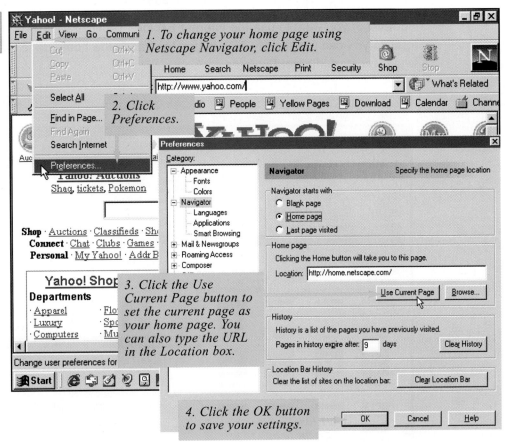

■ If you decide not to use Netscape Home as your home page, you might want to return to http://home.netscape.com occasionally to check for updates and information about the Netscape Navigator browser.

■ How do I change my home page? (continued)

Your AOL software is configured to display a special AOL home page every time that you connect. When this book was written, the home page setting did not change the page that appears when you first connect to AOL or the first page that appears when you click AOL's *Go To the Internet* option. AOL is constantly updating its software, so this behavior might be different in the future.

However, if you want to use the Internet Explorer browser while you are connected to AOL, you can use the My AOL button to change the home page that appears when you start Internet Explorer.

AOL

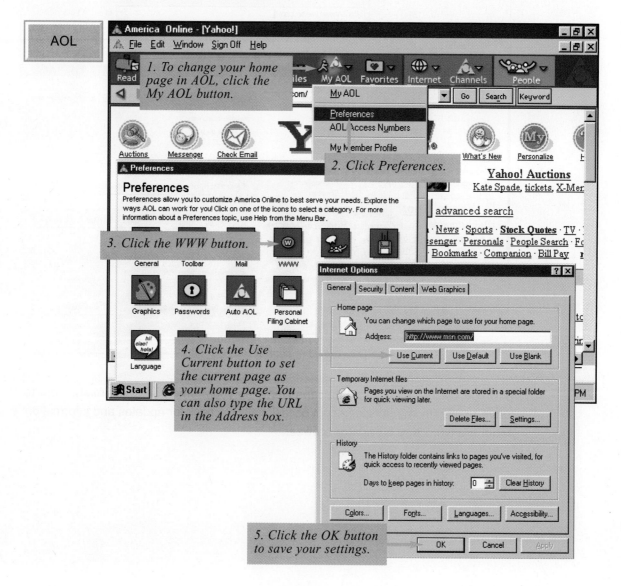

1. To change your home page in AOL, click the My AOL button.

2. Click Preferences.

3. Click the WWW button.

4. Click the Use Current button to set the current page as your home page. You can also type the URL in the Address box.

5. Click the OK button to save your settings.

QuickCheck A

1. A(n) [_____] such as www.yahoo.com/automobiles or www.msu.edu/fac, uniquely defines a particular Web page.

2. When you start a browser, it automatically loads and displays a page from a Web site. This starting page is known as your [_____].

3. Assume that you typed a URL in order to go to Web page A, then you clicked a link to go to Web page B. If you click the Back button, then click the Forward button, page [_____] will be displayed on your screen.

4. True or false? Favorites and Bookmarks are essentially the same thing. [_____]

5. True or false? The History list shows only Web pages that you visited during the current computing session. [_____]

Check It!

QuickCheck B

Indicate the letter of the browser element that best matches the following:

1. The button that displays the previous page [____]

2. The button that displays your home page [____]

3. The button to click if a page takes too long to load [____]

4. A text link [____]

5. A graphics link [____]

Check It!

Get It?

[A] Skill Set A: Using Internet Explorer

[C] Skill Set C: Using AOL

[B] Skill Set B: Using Netscape

Chapter 3

Exploring the Web

What's Inside?

As soon as you've mastered the basic skills necessary for using your browser, you'll want to begin to explore everything that the Web has to offer. In this chapter, you'll have an opportunity to try the Web's most popular activities. First, you'll do a little bit of online shopping and participate in an online auction to learn about **e-commerce**. Next, you'll find out how to get free software, music, plug-ins, and players from Web sites. You'll also find out how to create and post your own Web pages.

While you explore the Web, it is important to remain vigilant about security and privacy. This chapter ends with some tips about avoiding Web-borne viruses, keeping your Web activities private, and monitoring your children's Internet usage.

∎FAQ How do I purchase merchandise online?

Online shopping is similar to using a mail-order catalog, except that instead of selecting merchandise from a catalog, you browse through a merchant's Web site that contains product descriptions, photos, and prices. When you locate something that you want to buy, you add it to your online **shopping cart**, which is a list of items that you want to purchase.

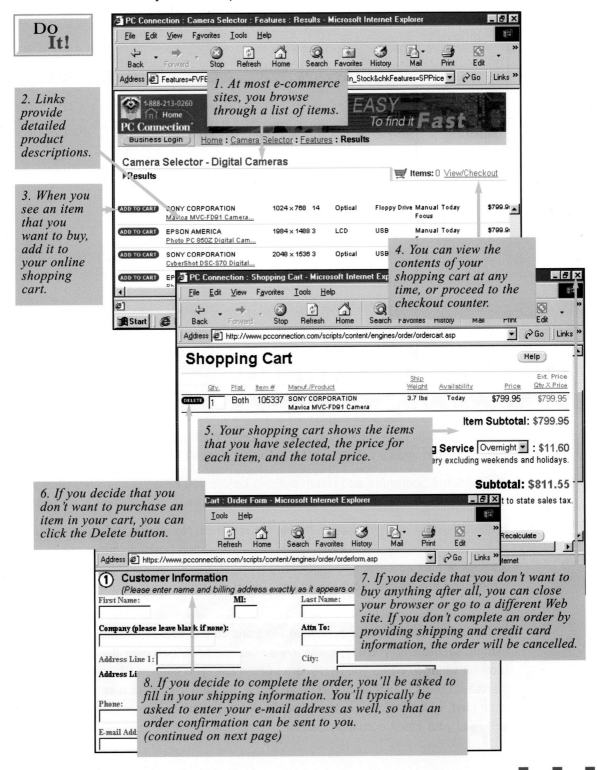

Do It!

2. Links provide detailed product descriptions.

3. When you see an item that you want to buy, add it to your online shopping cart.

1. At most e-commerce sites, you browse through a list of items.

4. You can view the contents of your shopping cart at any time, or proceed to the checkout counter.

5. Your shopping cart shows the items that you have selected, the price for each item, and the total price.

6. If you decide that you don't want to purchase an item in your cart, you can click the Delete button.

7. If you decide that you don't want to buy anything after all, you can close your browser or go to a different Web site. If you don't complete an order by providing shipping and credit card information, the order will be cancelled.

8. If you decide to complete the order, you'll be asked to fill in your shipping information. You'll typically be asked to enter your e-mail address as well, so that an order confirmation can be sent to you.
(continued on next page)

■ How do I purchase merchandise online? (continued)

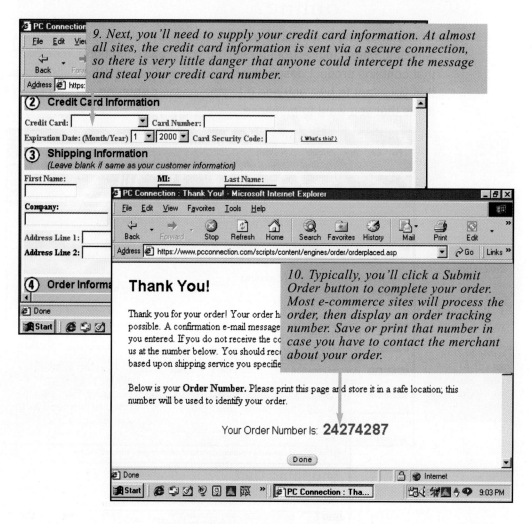

9. Next, you'll need to supply your credit card information. At almost all sites, the credit card information is sent via a secure connection, so there is very little danger that anyone could intercept the message and steal your credit card number.

10. Typically, you'll click a Submit Order button to complete your order. Most e-commerce sites will process the order, then display an order tracking number. Save or print that number in case you have to contact the merchant about your order.

■ Most e-commerce sites display an order confirmation number or e-mail a copy of the invoice to you. You should save the order confirmation number or print the invoice so that you can check on the order if it doesn't arrive when expected.

■ Check the guarantee and return policies before you order. Some Web sites have limited return and replacement policies.

■ Don't provide any information that is not required. No site should ask for your social security number or for other personal information beyond your name, address, e-mail address, and credit card number. Usually the boxes for required information are marked so that you know what information is really necessary to process the order.

■ Most sites use a secure connection to transmit financial information. When using a secure link, you'll typically see a small padlock icon near the bottom of the browser window. When you're using a secure link, you might notice that the URL starts with https:// instead of the usual http://. All data sent over a secure link is encrypted, which makes it extremely difficult for anyone to intercept the message and read your credit card information.

■FAQ How do online auctions work?

You can think of **online auction sites** such as eBay, as the world's largest flea markets or garage sales. People from all over the world list items for sale and take bids for these items. Bids are accepted only for a specified time period—usually about seven days. If you find an item that you would like to purchase, you can enter a bid for that item. If you are the highest bidder at the end of the auction, you send your payment to the seller, and then the seller sends the item to you.

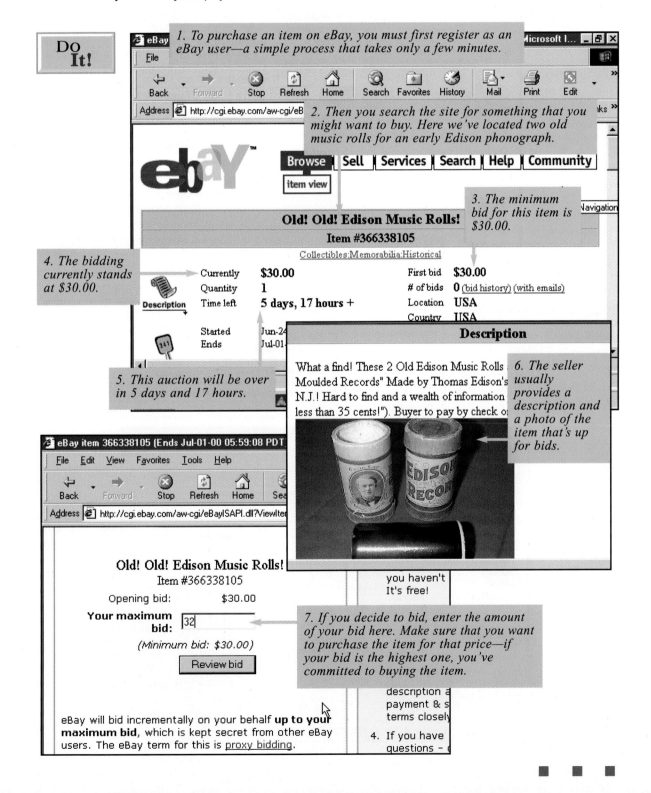

Do It!

1. *To purchase an item on eBay, you must first register as an eBay user—a simple process that takes only a few minutes.*

2. *Then you search the site for something that you might want to buy. Here we've located two old music rolls for an early Edison phonograph.*

3. *The minimum bid for this item is $30.00.*

4. *The bidding currently stands at $30.00.*

5. *This auction will be over in 5 days and 17 hours.*

6. *The seller usually provides a description and a photo of the item that's up for bids.*

7. *If you decide to bid, enter the amount of your bid here. Make sure that you want to purchase the item for that price—if your bid is the highest one, you've committed to buying the item.*

■ How do online auctions work? (continued)

You can sell your own antiques, heirlooms, and collectibles through an online auction. To sell an item, you must first register with the auction site. Once you have done so, you can enter information describing the item that you're selling and you can set the terms for the auction.

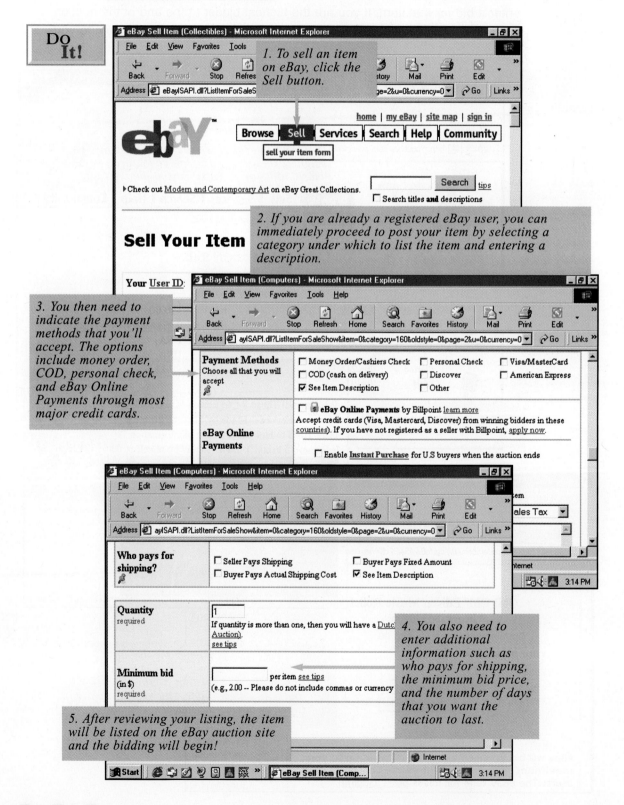

Do It!

1. To sell an item on eBay, click the Sell button.

2. If you are already a registered eBay user, you can immediately proceed to post your item by selecting a category under which to list the item and entering a description.

3. You then need to indicate the payment methods that you'll accept. The options include money order, COD, personal check, and eBay Online Payments through most major credit cards.

4. You also need to enter additional information such as who pays for shipping, the minimum bid price, and the number of days that you want the auction to last.

5. After reviewing your listing, the item will be listed on the eBay auction site and the bidding will begin!

■ How do online auctions work? (continued)

On the previous pages, you've seen how to buy and sell items at an online auction. You might, however, have a few questions about the process including "How do I know that the seller will ship the item?" and "How do I know that the product is what the seller said it was?". Of the thousands of online fraud complaints handled by the National Consumer's League each year, more than 80% concern online auctions. Although, many auction sites provide some insurance against fraud (eBay on purchases up to $200 and Amazon.com on purchases up to $1,000), this insurance only covers transactions in which the item is never delivered. If the item is not "as advertised" or if you are simply not satisfied with an item, you may have little recourse. To deal with the issue of trust, online auctions have developed vendor rating systems and escrow services.

A **vendor rating system** provides "report cards" on the performance of individuals or businesses that have offered items for sale at an auction site. These performance ratings are compiled from comments made by customers who have purchased merchandise from a vendor's previous auctions. Typically, high ratings mean that customers have been satisfied with the quality of the merchandise and that items arrived promptly and in good condition. Before you bid at an online auction, it is a good idea to check the vendor's rating—especially when bidding on an expensive item.

An **escrow service** is a financial business that charges a small fee to act as an intermediary between a buyer and a seller. Both the buyer and the seller register with the escrow service and supply credit card information. The seller deposits the payment for an item with the escrow service, which holds the payment until the buyer receives the item. If the item arrives and it is satisfactory, the escrow service releases the payment to the vendor. If the item is not satisfactory, the buyer can ask the escrow service to hold the payment until an acceptable solution can be negotiated.

■ Prices at online auctions are not always lower than the prices you might find at a local garage sale. Make sure that you do your homework to determine an appropriate price before you place your bid.

■ Don't get carried away with the excitement of the bidding process. Know what you're willing to pay before you start. If the bids exceed that price, be prepared to let the item go to another bidder.

■ Don't place a bid unless you are ready and able to purchase the product for that price. When you place a bid, you are entering into a contract to purchase the item at that price, if you are the highest bidder.

■ Special software is available that allows you to spy on an auction and place a bid just before the end of the auction period. Most of the online auction sites try to discourage or prevent the use of this software because it disrupts the auction process if someone places a bid for ten cents over your bid in the closing seconds of the auction.

■ You'll find online auctions at www.ebay.com and www.amazon.com, as well as at many portal sites.

■FAQ How do I download software, music, and other files?

Many Web sites offer a variety of music, software, photo, and data files that you can download to your computer. The term **download** simply means to transmit a file from a remote computer, such as a Web server, to your own computer. Downloading software from a Web site is fairly easy. Look for a "Download" link or button, then click it to start the download process. You'll need to specify the drive and folder in which you want to store the downloaded file.

If you download a data file such as an MP3 music file or a document, you'll need to open the file with an appropriate application program. In the case of an MP3 music file, you'll need to open it using an MP3 player. To view a document, open it with a word processing program such as Microsoft Word.

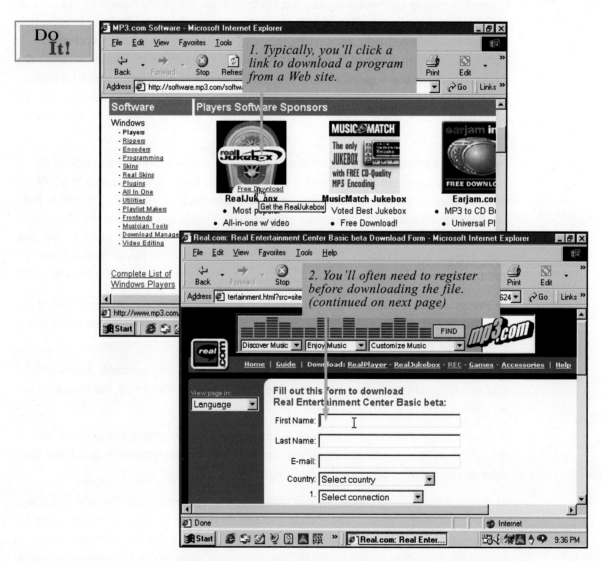

Do It!

1. Typically, you'll click a link to download a program from a Web site.

2. You'll often need to register before downloading the file. (continued on next page)

■ How do I download software, music, and other files? (continued)

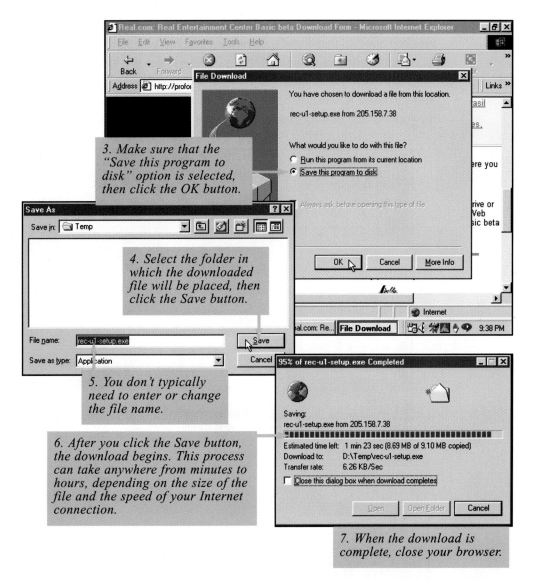

3. Make sure that the "Save this program to disk" option is selected, then click the OK button.

4. Select the folder in which the downloaded file will be placed, then click the Save button.

5. You don't typically need to enter or change the file name.

6. After you click the Save button, the download begins. This process can take anywhere from minutes to hours, depending on the size of the file and the speed of your Internet connection.

7. When the download is complete, close your browser.

■ Make sure that you remember or write down the drive, folder, and file name where you've stored a downloaded file, so that you'll be able to locate it and use it in the future.

■ Many companies provide free trial versions of their software. You can typically download this software from their Web sites, install it, and then use it for a limited period of time. If you like the software, you can then usually purchase a license to continue using it. Just be aware that the free, trial versions of many programs are very large, and can require hours to download over a dial-up connection.

■ Some files that you'll download have been compressed or zipped to increase transfer speed. You'll find out how to work with these files in Chapter 7.

■ Check the file size before you start the download process. Many Web sites provide file sizes and estimated download times. If the file is really huge, you might find out if you can get it delivered via surface mail on a CD-ROM.

■ ■ ■

■ How do I download software, music, and other files? (continued)

When you download *software* (as opposed to downloading a program), you will typically need to install the software before you can use it. The installation program is included with the downloaded file. Sometimes, the installation program is configured to start automatically, as soon as the download is complete. In other cases, you will need to use the Start menu's Run command to locate the downloaded file on your computer and manually start the installation program.

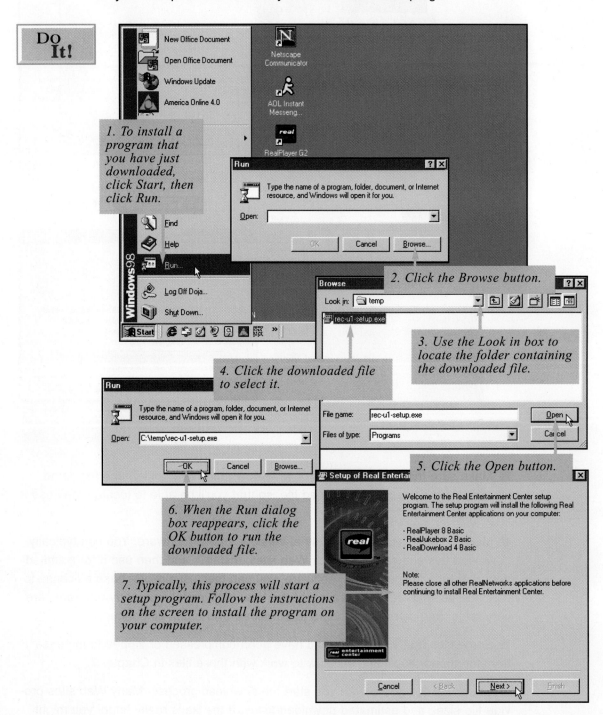

1. To install a program that you have just downloaded, click Start, then click Run.

2. Click the Browse button.

3. Use the Look in box to locate the folder containing the downloaded file.

4. Click the downloaded file to select it.

5. Click the Open button.

6. When the Run dialog box reappears, click the OK button to run the downloaded file.

7. Typically, this process will start a setup program. Follow the instructions on the screen to install the program on your computer.

■FAQ What about plug-ins and players?

Many Web pages incorporate media elements such as streaming video or music files. If you try to view a media element and nothing happens or an error message appears, then you probably need to download the latest version of a plug-in or player. A **plug-in** or **player** is an add-on program that enables your browser to access Web media elements, such as streaming videos, Flash animations, 360 degree movies, or MP3 music.

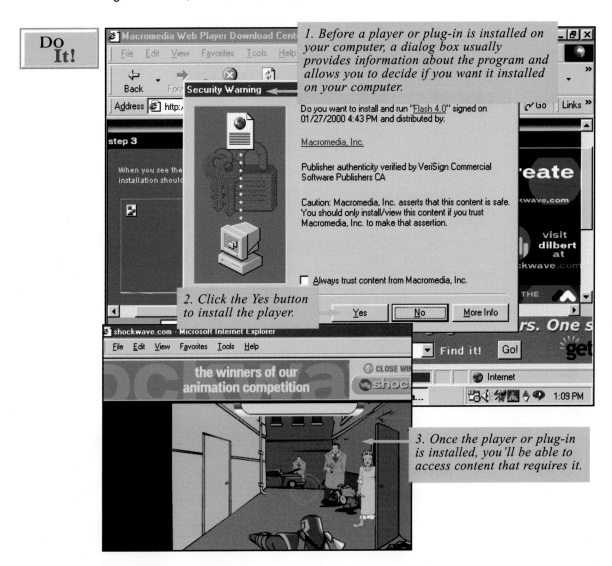

Do It!

1. Before a player or plug-in is installed on your computer, a dialog box usually provides information about the program and allows you to decide if you want it installed on your computer.

2. Click the Yes button to install the player.

3. Once the player or plug-in is installed, you'll be able to access content that requires it.

■ The Microsoft Media Player from www.microsoft.com, and the RealMedia Player from www.real.com, provide support for streaming video and music files.

■ The Macromedia Shockwave player, available at http://sdc.shockwave.com/, allows your browser to display ShockWave and Flash animations used at many Web sites.

■ The Adobe Acrobat plug-in, available at www.adobe.com, allows you to view and print fully formatted PDF files of technical service manuals, product specification sheets, and similar documents.

■ ■ ■

■FAQ How can I create my own Web page?

A Web page is a document that's formatted by embedding special **HTML** (Hyper-text Markup Language) "tags" to specify text color, background color, font type, font size, and the position of links and graphics. These tags are interpreted by a browser to, for example, display black text on a light beige background.

A wide variety of Web page creation tools are available. Many ISPs, including America Online, provide such tools. You probably have an easy-to-use Web page creation tool already installed on your computer—Microsoft Word. One of the easiest ways to produce a basic Web page is to create a document in Microsoft Word, then use the Save as Web Page feature to convert the document into HTML format.

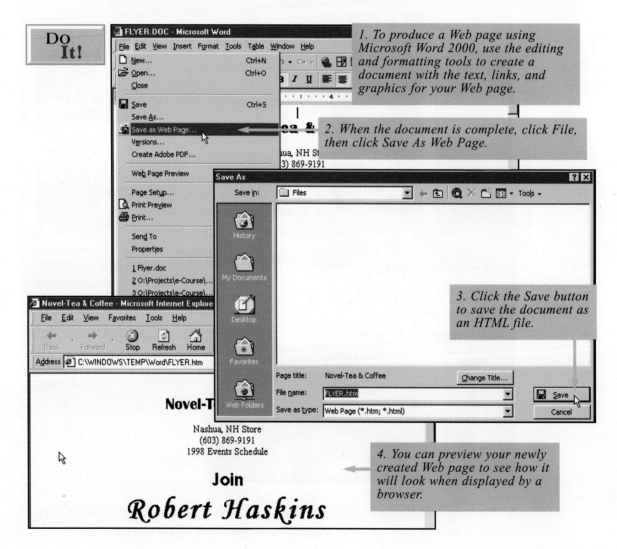

1. To produce a Web page using Microsoft Word 2000, use the editing and formatting tools to create a document with the text, links, and graphics for your Web page.

2. When the document is complete, click File, then click Save As Web Page.

3. Click the Save button to save the document as an HTML file.

4. You can preview your newly created Web page to see how it will look when displayed by a browser.

■ Not all of Word's formatting features can be successfully converted into HTML tags. Headers and footers for example, will typically not be formatted correctly. After converting a document into HTML format, make sure that you preview it in a browser and check that all of the text and graphics are displayed as expected.

■ How can I create my own Web page? (continued)

Microsoft Word is fine for simple Web pages, but it's less than ideal for more complex Web sites. If you need more control over the format of your Web page, or if you want to create a sophisticated Web site with multiple pages and navigation bars, then you should consider using a specialized Web page development tool such as Microsoft FrontPage.

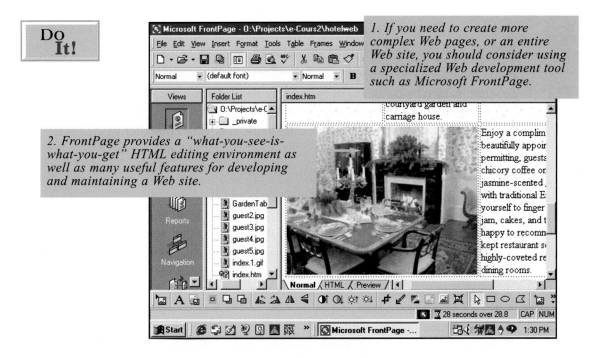

1. If you need to create more complex Web pages, or an entire Web site, you should consider using a specialized Web development tool such as Microsoft FrontPage.

2. FrontPage provides a "what-you-see-is-what-you-get" HTML editing environment as well as many useful features for developing and maintaining a Web site.

You can use the Windows Notepad to create an HTML document "from scratch." You can also directly edit the HTML tags that exist in FrontPage files or in files that were converted into HTML format by Microsoft Word.

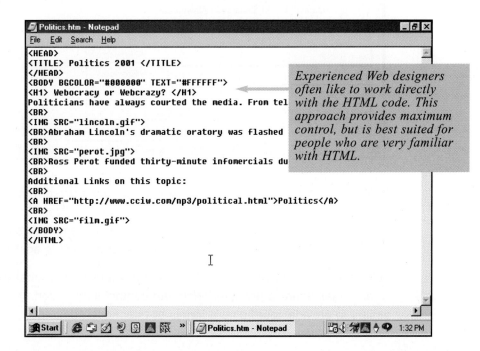

Experienced Web designers often like to work directly with the HTML code. This approach provides maximum control, but is best suited for people who are very familiar with HTML.

■FAQ Where can I post my Web page after I've created it?

After you've created a Web page or a Web site, you will need to post it on a Web server so that other people can access it. Many ISPs and portal sites provide Web server space where subscribers and members can post their Web pages without charge. Schools, colleges, and universities may also provide server space for faculty and student Web pages. Web hosting services, such as www.verio.com, charge a monthly fee for server space, but also offer site management and e-commerce features that are great if you want to get your business online.

If you create your Web page with an online Web creation tool such as the Yahoo! program shown below, it will automatically be placed on the Web server for you. If you create a Web page with a program such as Microsoft Word or Microsoft Front-Page, you will need to transfer the Web page from your computer to the Web server—a process called **uploading**. Instructions for uploading Web pages are generally included in the online Help system at the posting site.

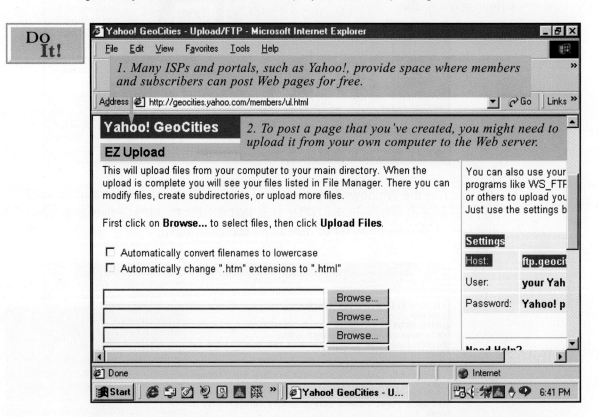

Do It!

1. Many ISPs and portals, such as Yahoo!, provide space where members and subscribers can post Web pages for free.

2. To post a page that you've created, you might need to upload it from your own computer to the Web server.

■ You should remember that when a Web page is posted to a Web server, it can be reached by anyone in the world with access to the Web. Students in particular should remember that their parents and prospective employers might be among those who visit their sites—make sure that your content is appropriate.

■ Consider your privacy and safety when composing personal Web pages. Usually, an e-mail address provides adequate contact information. It is usually not necessary to provide your home address or telephone number.

■FAQ Can visiting a Web site cause damage to my computer?

Most Web sites consist of pages containing HTML tags, which are limited to "safe" functions such as changing fonts and colors. Some Web pages also include "scripts," written in JavaScript or VBScript, that add interactivity to pages. Web pages that contain HTML and scripts cannot typically cause damage to your computer by spreading a virus or erasing files.

To provide features that go beyond the limits of HTML and scripts, many Web sites incorporate Java and ActiveX components. These components are written using full-featured programming languages that include commands for copying and erasing files. A malicious programmer could create a Web page containing a Java program or ActiveX component that could attempt to copy files from your computer, erase files, or cause other problems. To minimize the possibility of receiving a malicious Java or ActiveX component, most browsers can be configured to display a message alerting you when a Web page contains one of these components. You can then decide whether to accept the component and run it.

How do you know whether a component is "safe"? Legitimate components are usually "signed" and validated with a **digital certificate** issued by a certifying agency such as VeriSign. Before your browser runs a signed ActiveX component on your computer, it typically displays the certificate showing the name of the component and the person or company that created it. Signed components are likely to be safe, so you can tell your browser to accept the component and run it. You might, however, want to reject unsigned components.

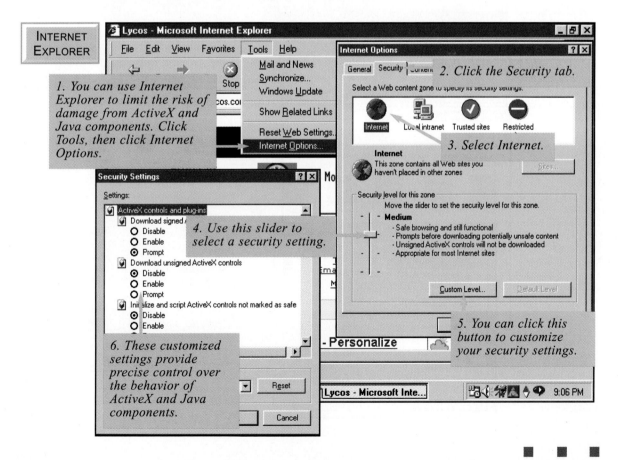

■ **Can visiting a Web site cause damage to my computer? (continued)**

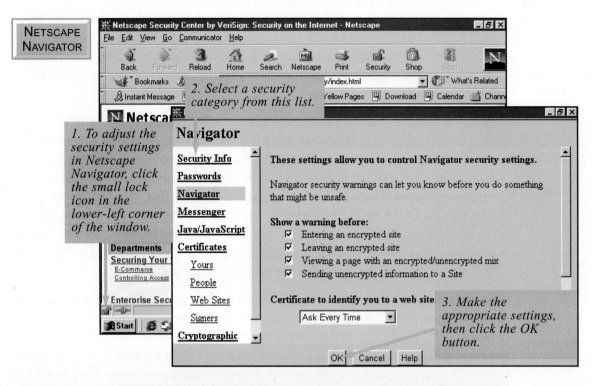

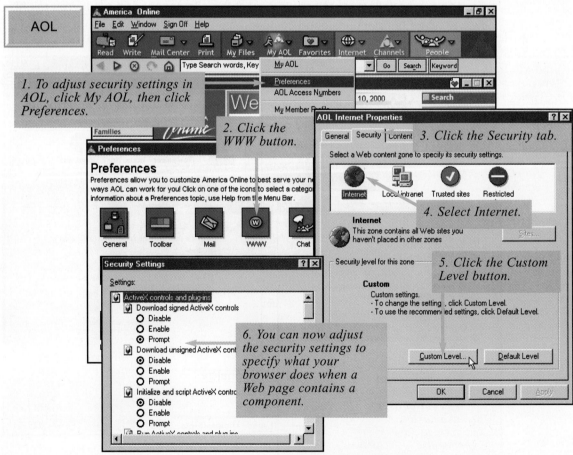

■FAQ Can other people find out which Web sites I've visited?

There are many reasons why you might not want other people to see which Web sites you visit. For example, you might be searching for information on a health-related issue that you would prefer to keep confidential. If you're using your browser at work to look for a new job, you might not want your boss or colleagues to know about your plans.

Each time that you visit a Web page, the title and URL for the page are recorded in the History list of your browser. Anyone with access to your computer can easily check this list to track your path through cyberspace. In addition to the History list, Windows stores a group of files in the Windows\Temporary Internet Files folder of your computer's hard disk. These temporary files also display the titles and URLs of Web pages that you've visited. To hide your tracks in cyberspace, you'll need to clear the History list and delete the temporary Internet files. Your browser provides a way to do so.

Internet Explorer's Tools menu provides an easy way to clear the History list and delete the temporary Internet files that provide clues to the Web pages that you have visited.

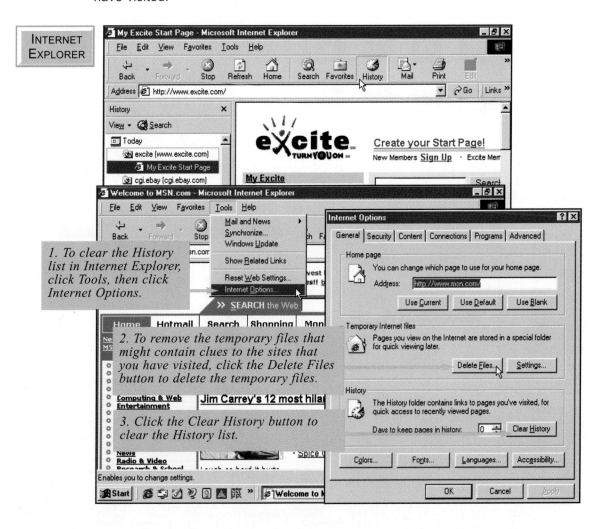

INTERNET
EXPLORER

1. To clear the History list in Internet Explorer, click Tools, then click Internet Options.

2. To remove the temporary files that might contain clues to the sites that you have visited, click the Delete Files button to delete the temporary files.

3. Click the Clear History button to clear the History list.

■ Can other people find out which Web sites I've visited? (continued)

Like Internet Explorer, the AOL browser provides an easy way to clear the History list and delete the temporary Internet files on your computer. Netscape Navigator, however, allows you to clear the History list, but does not provide an easy way to delete temporary Internet files.

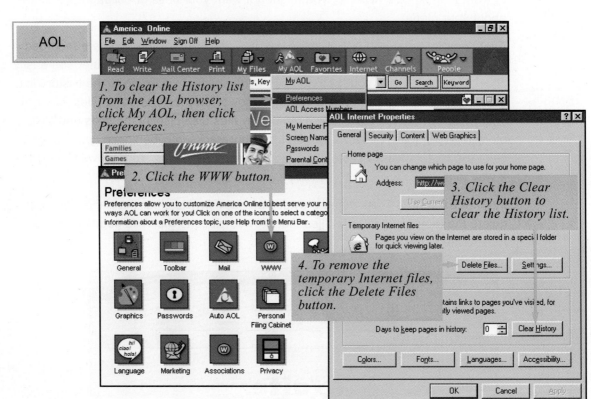

AOL

1. To clear the History list from the AOL browser, click My AOL, then click Preferences.

2. Click the WWW button.

3. Click the Clear History button to clear the History list.

4. To remove the temporary Internet files, click the Delete Files button.

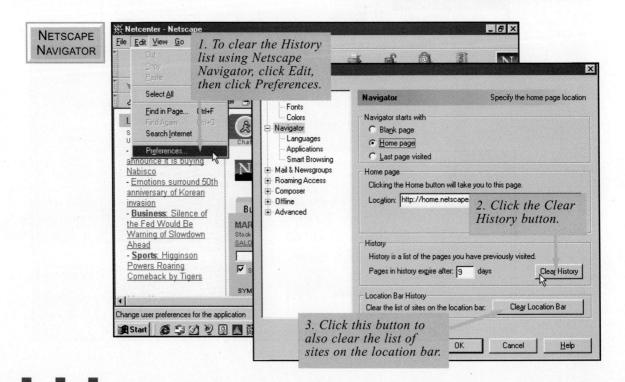

NETSCAPE NAVIGATOR

1. To clear the History list using Netscape Navigator, click Edit, then click Preferences.

2. Click the Clear History button.

3. Click this button to also clear the list of sites on the location bar.

■ Can other people find out which Web sites I've visited? (continued)

Even if you clear the History list and delete the temporary Internet files, a collection of files, called "cookies," remains on your computer. A **cookie** is a small file that is stored on your computer by a Web server. Each cookie contains information that identifies you and that can help a Web server customize Web pages for your interests. If you're really serious about protecting your online privacy, you should locate and delete these files from your computer on a regular basis. Note, however, that after you've cleared these files, sites that have previously given you a cookie won't know that you're a repeat visitor. If your cookie was storing preferences, you'll have to reselect them the next time that you visit the site.

Cookies are stored in a Windows subfolder called Cookies. They are also stored in the Windows subfolder called Temporary Internet Files. Regardless of which browser you use, you can view a list of cookie files using Windows Explorer. You can then delete some or all of the cookies.

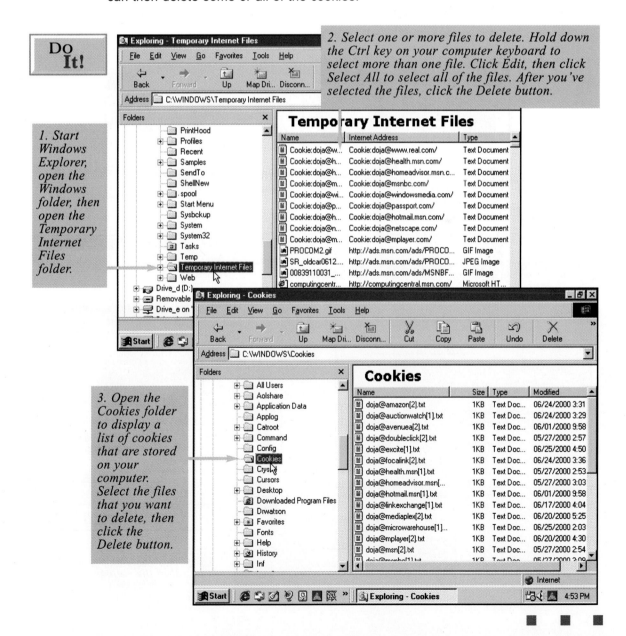

Do It!

1. Start Windows Explorer, open the Windows folder, then open the Temporary Internet Files folder.

2. Select one or more files to delete. Hold down the Ctrl key on your computer keyboard to select more than one file. Click Edit, then click Select All to select all of the files. After you've selected the files, click the Delete button.

3. Open the Cookies folder to display a list of cookies that are stored on your computer. Select the files that you want to delete, then click the Delete button.

■FAQ How do I prevent my children from reaching objectionable Web sites?

The Web encompasses sites devoted to just about every topic, including many that parents would not find appropriate for their children. Today's browsers allow parents to filter out Web sites that contain adult language, nudity, sex, or violence. The settings for a browser filter are controlled by a password. Keep this password confidential so that your children will not be able to change the settings.

Filters are based on ratings provided voluntarily by every Web site. A voluntary rating system is not necessarily thorough or accurate, however, so it is a good idea to periodically check on your children's Internet sessions. If you want more versatile filtering capabilities than your browser provides, you might try a commercial filtering program, available from Web sites such as www.cybersitter.com, www.surfwatch.com, or www.netnanny.com.

Internet Explorer's Content Advisor allows you to easily filter sites that contain adult language, nudity, sex, and violence.

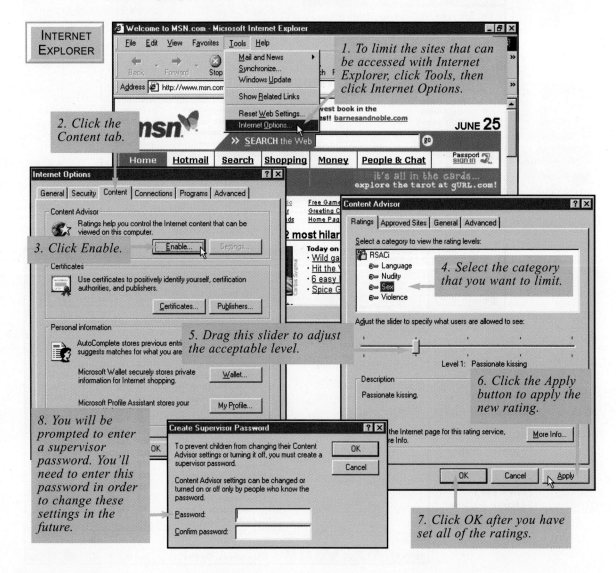

■ How do I prevent my children from reaching objectionable Web sites? (continued)

Netscape Navigator's NetWatch utility allows you to filter Web sites based on ratings provided voluntarily by Web site publishers. To make NetWatch settings, you must be online.

NETSCAPE
NAVIGATOR

1. To limit access in Netscape, connect to the Internet, click Help, then click NetWatch.

2. Click here to set up NetWatch.

Netscape NetWatch

NetWatch is Netscape Navigator's built-in ratings protection feature. It lets you control what kind of web pages can be viewed on your computer.

click to set up NetWatch

PICS Ratings Standard

Set acceptable levels (0 for the greatest protection, 4 for the least protection):

Language   0 No offensive language
Violence   0 No violence or sports-related violence only
Nudity   0 No nudity
Sex
0 No nudity
1 Revealing attire
2 Partial nudity
3 Frontal nudity
4 Provocative display of frontal nudity

3. Set the acceptable level for each category.

■ How do I prevent my children from reaching objectionable Web sites? (continued)

In both Internet Explorer and Netscape Navigator, filters apply to everyone who uses the browser on that computer. You cannot, therefore, select one setting for younger children and a different setting for older children or adults. America Online provides a more versatile set of parental controls. You can specify different settings for each screen name, which means that you can select a different level of access for younger children, older children, and adults.

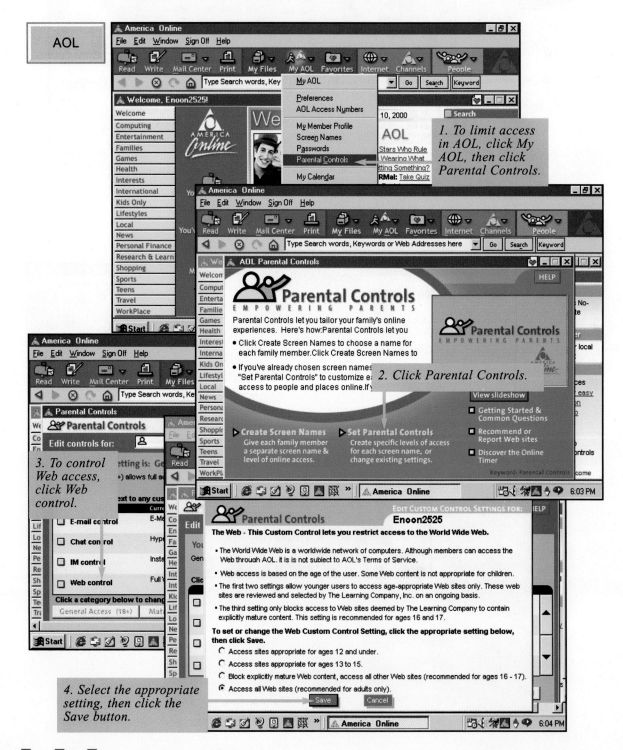

QuickCheck A

1. True or false? Most e-commerce sites use secure connections, so there is very little chance of your credit card information being intercepted. ☐

2. An online ☐ is like a gigantic garage sale, where people around the world can buy and sell items.

3. True or false? If you use your browser to clear the History list and delete the temporary Internet files, no traces will remain of the Web sites that you have visited. ☐

4. It is theoretically possible for a Web site to contain Java programs or ☐ components that could be designed to read or delete files on your computer.

5. A(n) ☐ or player is an add-on program that works with your browser to access specialized Web content such as streaming videos or music.

Check It!

QuickCheck B

Indicate the letter of the Web page element that you would click to:

1. Display a product description ☐

2. Add the Epson America Photo PC 850Z to your shopping cart ☐

3. Display the number of items in your shopping cart ☐

4. Look at other merchandise categories ☐

5. View the contents of your shopping cart ☐

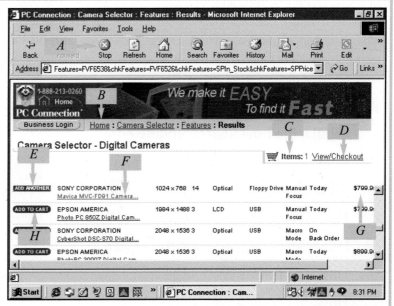

Check It!

Get It?

 Skill Set A: Purchasing Merchandise Online

C Skill Set C: Downloading Software

 Skill Set B: Bidding at an Online Auction

D Skill Set D: Creating a Web Page

Chapter 4

Searching for Information

What's Inside?

The Web encompasses information on virtually every topic, but how do you sift through hundreds of millions of Web pages to find specific information? In this chapter, you'll learn techniques for locating useful information on the Web. You'll also learn how to save information and graphics that you've found, plus how to incorporate this information in documents that you produce.

When looking for specific information, most people first turn to a search engine. A **search engine** is an Internet-based program that compiles an extensive index of keywords and the URLs for the Web pages on which those words can be found. Many search engines send out automated software agents called **spiders** to continually prowl from one Web site to another, looking for new additions to the index. A spider starts at one Web page, and then follows every link on that page, collecting URLs for keywords as it goes along. Methodically following links, a Web crawler can eventually identify and index millions—or even billions—of Web pages.

At a search engine Web site, you can access an index of Web pages by entering one or more keywords. Many search engine sites also provide a hierarchical list of topics that you can use to "drill down" to a specific subject. Some sites even provide the online equivalent of a human research assistant that will answer queries entered as simple questions, such as "Where can I find the blue book price of a '92 Blazer?"

- FAQs:

■FAQ What's the best search engine?

All of the popular search engines index millions of Web pages. However, each search engine uses different indexing and user interface technologies, so different search engines can give you very different results. You might consider using more than one search engine—especially for particularly tricky searches.

AltaVista (www.altavista.com) allows you to enter keywords or drill down through a hierarchy of topics presented in a category list. It has gained a reputation as a search site that appeals to a widely diverse set of users.

Ask Jeeves (www.ask.com) is operated by the same company as AltaVista, but it specializes in "natural language" queries. Instead of entering a keyword, you can enter a specific question, such as "What's the best low-cost notebook computer?". Jeeves will produce a list of relevant Web sites—perhaps some links to product reviews—and also offer links to general computer information and shopping sites.

Excite (www.excite.com) allows you to search by keyword or by using a category list. In addition to a search engine, Excite provides many news and chat links, making it a good portal site.

The **FAST** (www.alltheweb.com) search engine was formerly called "All the Web," which accounts for its URL. A relative newcomer to the roster of search engines, FAST specializes in targeted searches by allowing you to formulate a search for a specific product within categories for downloadable software, music, or multimedia.

Google (www.google.com), started in 1999, quickly gained popularity because it was the first search engine to index over one billion Web pages. Google specializes in keyword searches and even features an "I'm feeling lucky" button that returns only one link—theoretically the only site you'll need to visit to find the information that you are seeking. Google rates each Web page by the number of times a page has been accessed and tends to place links for frequently accessed pages first in the list of search results. Unlike many other search engines, Google has not allowed companies to purchase a high placement in the list of search results.

Lycos (www.lycos.com) is one of the oldest search engine and portal sites on the Web. It has a reputation for being an excellent tool for accessing technical information, although its index includes everything from Art to Travel.

NorthernLight (www.northernlight.com) is unique in the way that it organizes your search results. In addition to the usual long list of Web sites that are relevant to a query, NorthernLight organizes search results into a number of folders. For example, the results of a search for "pine cone quilt" might be organized into folders such as Hobbies & Crafts, Quilting, Antiques, and Home Decor, allowing you to focus your search on the links in the most relevant category.

Yahoo! (www.yahoo.com) is consistently rated as one of the most popular search engines and portal sites. It is the largest human-compiled guide to the Web. Over 150 editors and research assistants continually update Yahoo!'s extensive category listing that allows you to easily narrow your search on a specific topic.

■   ■   ■

■FAQ How do I use a search engine?

To perform a **keyword search**, you enter a word or series of words in a search box. Be as specific as possible. A keyword search for "Ford" will turn up thousands of pages about Ford automobiles, as well as pages about former president Gerald Ford and actor Harrison Ford. "Ford automobile" would result in a much more targeted search and return a more manageable number of results.

1. For a keyword search, you typically enter one or more keywords into a search box.

2. Then, click a button or press the Enter key to initiate the search.

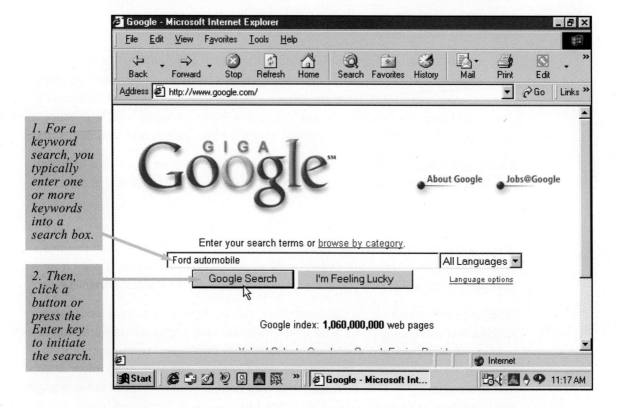

When you enter more than one keyword, your browser interprets your request as "Show me links to Web pages that contain *any* of the words that I have typed in the Search box"—the words "Ford" or "automobile" in the example above. At the top of the list of results, a search engine displays links to pages that contain both the terms "Ford" and "automobile." After exhausting those pages, however, it displays links to pages that contain only the word "Ford." Another batch of links might contain only the word "automobile."

Search engines provide you with tools to make your searches more specific. These tools vary somewhat, depending on which search engine you're using, but are explained in detail somewhere on the search engine Web site. In general, a search engine will provide tools for exact-phrase searches and Boolean searches.

An **exact-phrase search** requires the search engine to find pages that include a particular phrase with the words occurring in the specified order. For example, an exact-phrase search for "Model T Ford" should produce a list of Web pages containing precisely that phrase. The list should not contain links to pages about Ford model kits or the Model T Hotel and Casino. To specify an exact-phrase search, you typically surround the phrase with quotation marks.

■ How do I use a search engine? (continued)

A **Boolean search** uses the operators (or symbols) AND(+), OR, and NOT(-) to specify how your keywords are to be combined. For example, if a search for "Model T automobile" turns up a lot of pages about car clubs that don't interest you, you can refine your search by entering: "Model T automobile" -club. Using the minus sign before the word "club" indicates that you don't want to see links to any pages containing that word.

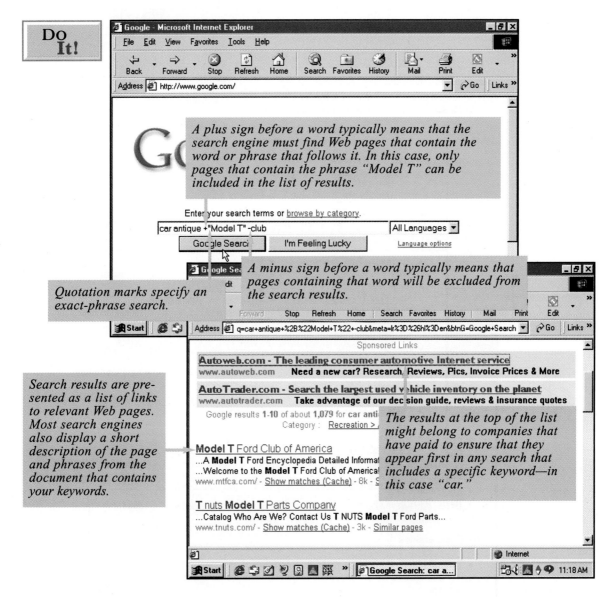

A plus sign before a word typically means that the search engine must find Web pages that contain the word or phrase that follows it. In this case, only pages that contain the phrase "Model T" can be included in the list of results.

Quotation marks specify an exact-phrase search.

A minus sign before a word typically means that pages containing that word will be excluded from the search results.

Search results are presented as a list of links to relevant Web pages. Most search engines also display a short description of the page and phrases from the document that contains your keywords.

The results at the top of the list might belong to companies that have paid to ensure that they appear first in any search that includes a specific keyword—in this case "car."

■ To connect to a Web site presented in the list of search results, simply click its underlined link. Although a search might produce thousands of links to Web pages, usually the first 20 or 30 links will provide the information that you need. If not, you should narrow your search by adding keywords, by using Boolean search techniques, or by creating an exact-phrase search.

■ How do I use a search engine? (continued)

In addition to keyword searches, some search sites also provide category links to help you locate information. A **category link** is a clickable word or phrase within a hierarchy of topics. To use category links, you make selections from lists of categories and subcategories until you reach a list of pages containing the information that you seek.

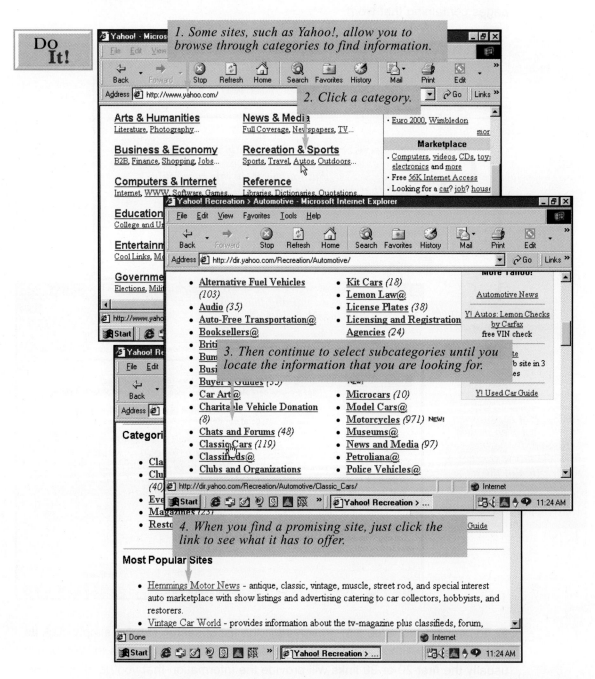

Do It!

1. Some sites, such as Yahoo!, allow you to browse through categories to find information.

2. Click a category.

3. Then continue to select subcategories until you locate the information that you are looking for.

4. When you find a promising site, just click the link to see what it has to offer.

■ The use of category links often leads to significantly different results than the use of a keyword search. If you can't find what you want through a keyword search, try the category links at Yahoo!.

■FAQ Where can I find links to news, sports, and weather on the Web?

You can use a search engine to find Web pages about a particular news item, a sports team, or weather patterns. It is often more efficient, however, to use targeted links at a portal site to access this type of general-interest information. If you find that you are using a portal site to repeatedly access a site about tropical weather, for example, you can add the site to your Favorites list.

Portal sites, such as Excite, provide search capabilities and links to specific topics including news, sports, and weather.

Most major news organizations have their own Web site such as this one at ABCNews.com.

■ Popular portal sites include www.excite.com, www.go.com, www.msn.com, www.yahoo.com, www.lycos.com, and www.aol.com.

■ Popular news sites include www.abcnews.com, www.msnbc.com, www.cbs.com, and www.cnn.com.

■ For the scoop on today's weather, try www.weather.com.

■FAQ How can I find people on the Web?

Various Web sites provide access to telephone listings throughout the U.S., Canada, much of Europe, and parts of Asia. You can use these listings to search for people, their phone numbers, and their addresses. It's a great way to get in touch with old classmates.

Do It!

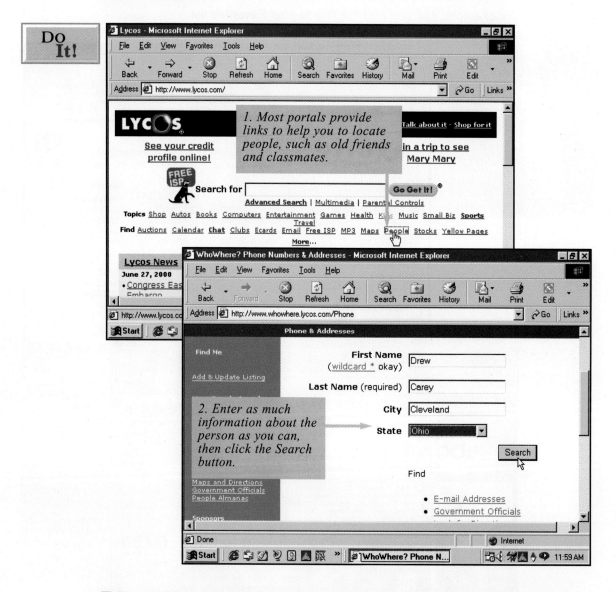

■ People with unusual names can be fairly easy to find, particularly if you know the city or state in which they live. People with common names such as John Smith can be more difficult to locate because your search might turn up hundreds, or even thousands, of people with that name.

■ To locate old classmates, you might try a site such as www.classmates.com, which allows you to search by name and school. Unfortunately, the databases at these sites are compiled from voluntary registrations, not from actual schools rosters, so many of your classmates may not be listed.

■FAQ How can I find places on the Web?

You can use the Web to get turn-by-turn driving directions and maps showing exactly how to get to a particular address or destination. As with most Web services, map and directions are free—all you need is a computer with a browser and an Internet connection.

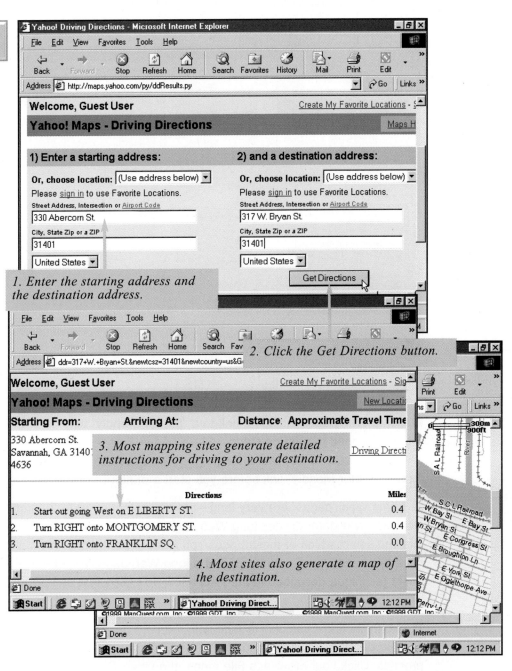

1. Enter the starting address and the destination address.

2. Click the Get Directions button.

3. Most mapping sites generate detailed instructions for driving to your destination.

4. Most sites also generate a map of the destination.

■ Would you like a detailed satellite photo of your house or land? Check out www.terraserver.com.

■ For additional maps, driving directions, and trip planning, try www.mapquest.com.

■FAQ How do I print a Web page?

Once you locate a Web page with relevant information, you might want to print it for future reference. Most browsers make it easy to print a Web page, typically by selecting File from the menu bar, then selecting Print.

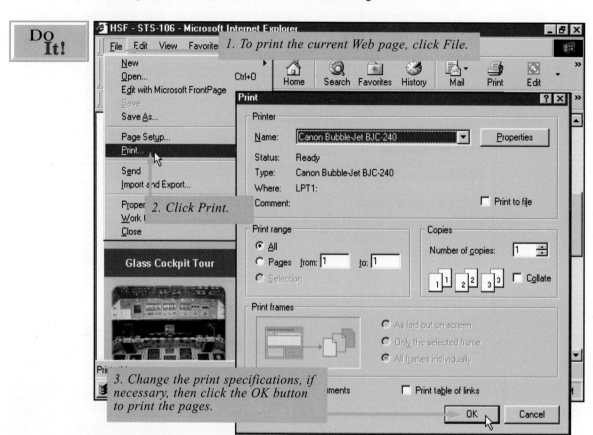

1. To print the current Web page, click File.

2. Click Print.

3. Change the print specifications, if necessary, then click the OK button to print the pages.

■ Some Web pages include a link to a "printer friendly" version of the Web page that is designed to print on standard size paper. This version is also designed to use color in such a way that a single page won't use all of your printer ink. Look for the "printer friendly" link before you start a printout.

■ Some Web "pages" are very long—the equivalent of 10 to 20 printed pages. Netscape Navigator divides long Web pages into a series of printable pages and lets you select which of those pages you want to print. Other browsers do not have this capability. To print a part of a long Web page, you can use the copy and paste technique described in the FAQ "How do I copy text and graphics from a Web page?"

■ You might find it useful to include both the Web page's URL and title as a header on your printout. You'll need to make this setting before you begin the print process. Click your browser's File menu, then click Page Setup. If you're using Internet Explorer, make sure that the Header box contains &w&u. If you are using Netscape, make sure that check marks appear next to *Document title* and *Document location*.

■FAQ How do I save a Web page?

You can easily save a Web page on your computer's hard disk, so that you can view it while you are offline. You can use the Save As option on your browser's File menu to initiate the save.

Most browsers give you the option of saving the page as an HTML file or as plain text. You should save the page as an HTML file if you want to use it as a Web page or view it in a browser. The file will include all of the HTML tags present in the original Web page. Alternatively, you can save the page as plain text and your browser will remove all of the embedded HTML tags. A plain text file is, therefore, easier to read if you open it with word processing software. It also works better than an HTML file if you want to later cut and paste text from the file into your own documents.

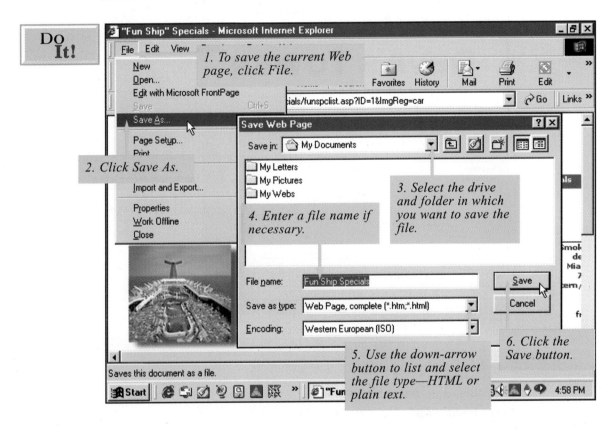

■ Depending on your browser, the graphics might not be included with the saved page. If the graphics are not saved with the page, you can save the graphics individually as explained in the next FAQ.

■FAQ How do I save a graphic from a Web page?

From time to time you'll run across graphics or photos that you'd like to save for future reference. You don't have to save the entire page on which the graphic appears, you can save just the graphic, storing it in its own file on your computer's hard disk. While viewing a Web page that contains a graphic that you want to save, right-click your mouse. A shortcut menu provides options for checking the graphic's file size and for saving it on your computer's hard disk.

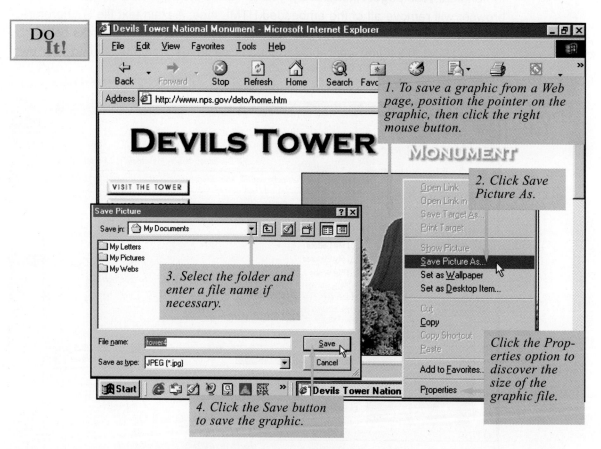

Do It!

1. To save a graphic from a Web page, position the pointer on the graphic, then click the right mouse button.

2. Click Save Picture As.

3. Select the folder and enter a file name if necessary.

Click the Properties option to discover the size of the graphic file.

4. Click the Save button to save the graphic.

■ In Netscape, the shortcut menu option is labeled "Save Image As" instead of "Save Picture As."

■ Most photos and pictures on the Web are copyrighted. You can usually save them for personal use, but should not use them in any commercial product or in your own Web pages unless you obtain permission from the copyright holder.

■ Most of the graphics that you see on Web pages exist as either JPEG or GIF files. Typically, these files are fairly small in size so that they travel quickly over the Internet and appear in your browser without much delay. You can use the Properties option on the shortcut menu to determine the size of a graphic.

■ Once you've saved a file on your computer, you can access it while offline by using your browser or any graphics software that opens JPEG and GIF files.

■FAQ How do I copy text and graphics from a Web page?

Suppose that you're searching the Web about a specific topic and taking notes for a research paper. It might be very useful to snip out a passage of text from a Web page and then paste it into the document that contains your notes. Later, when you compose the paper, you can incorporate the ideas from the passage or you can quote the passage in its entirety—including, of course, a reference citation to its source.

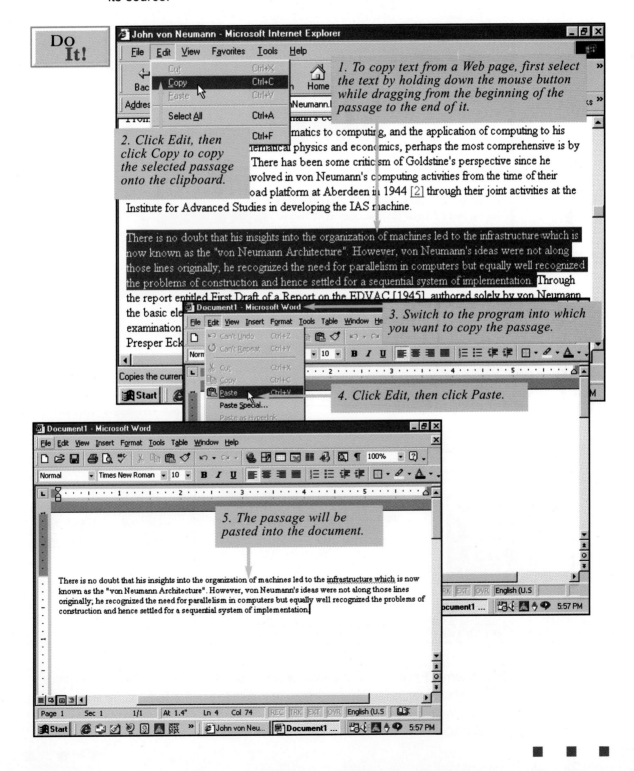

Do It!

1. To copy text from a Web page, first select the text by holding down the mouse button while dragging from the beginning of the passage to the end of it.

2. Click Edit, then click Copy to copy the selected passage onto the clipboard.

3. Switch to the program into which you want to copy the passage.

4. Click Edit, then click Paste.

5. The passage will be pasted into the document.

■ How do I copy text and graphics from a Web page? (continued)

In an earlier FAQ, you learned how to save a graphic from a Web page. As an alternative, you can simply copy a graphic from a Web page and paste it directly into a document. When you save the document, the graphic will be saved along with it.

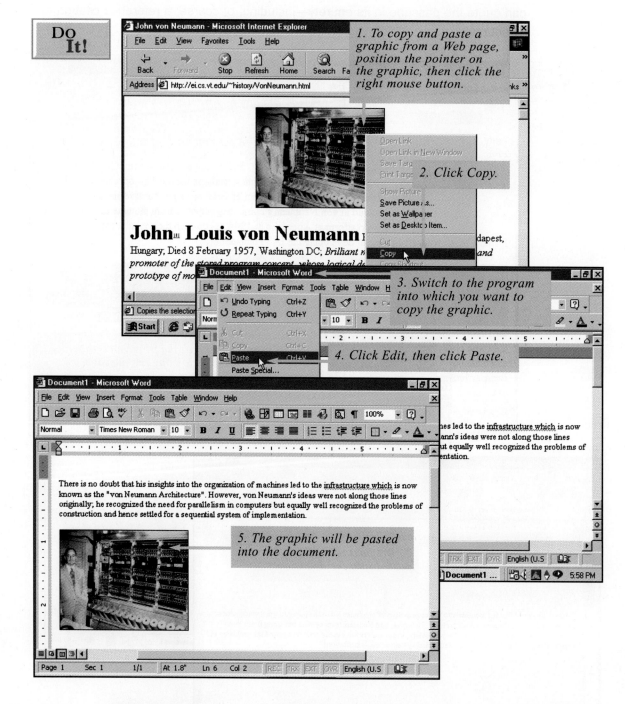

■ Both Internet Explorer and the AOL browser, provide a Copy option for graphics. Netscape Navigator, unfortunately, does not include such a feature. To work with a graphic while using Netscape Navigator, you'll need to save it as explained in the previous FAQ.

■FAQ what is the correct format for Web-based citations?

As with any other publications, the articles, photos, graphics, videos, software, and music that you find on the Web are typically protected by copyright laws. If you use any of this material in your own documents or Web pages, it is important to abide by copyright laws and respect the intellectual property rights of the original author or artist.

It is generally permissible to incorporate text and graphics that you find on the Web into your own documents. To avoid plagiarism, however, it is important to include a citation crediting the original source. A **citation**, also referred to as a "reference," provides your readers with information about the author of the original material and where that material can be found on the Web.

You might be familiar with citations for books—they include the author's name, book title, publisher and publication date. Citations can be placed in your document as footnotes on the bottom of each page, or as a works-cited list on the last page. The format and punctuation for citations, whether for books or for Web-based material, is specified in style manuals such as the *APA Publication Manual*, and the *MLA Style Manual*. The following examples, excerpted from the MLA Web site, illustrate the MLA citation style for a variety of different types of documents that can be found on the Web:

A citation for an individual's Web page:

Lancashire, Ian. Home page. 1 May 1997
<http://www.chass.utoronto.ca:8080/~ian/index.html>.

A citation for an article from an online magazine:

Landsburg, Steven E. "Who Shall Inherit the Earth?" Slate 1 May 1997. 2 May 1997 <http://www.slate.com/Economics/97-05-01/Economics.asp>.

A citation for material from a Compton's Encyclopedia article accessed through AOL:

"Table Tennis." Compton's Encyclopedia Online. Vers. 2.0. 1997. America Online. 4 July 1998. Keyword: Compton's.

■ For additional details on the citation format for material found on the Web, refer to the *APA Publication Manual* or the *MLA Style Manual*. You can also find information at the following Web sites:

http://www.mla.org/set_stl.htm

http://www.apa.org/journals/webref.html

■ What is the correct format for Web-based citations? (continued)

When you are searching the Web and taking notes for a research paper or report, you should make sure that you record the citation information along with your notes. If you forget to record the citation information, you might have a difficult time relocating the Web site when you are finalizing your document.

To simplify the process of gathering citation information, you can simply copy and paste document titles, author names, dates, and URLs from a Web document into the document that contains your notes.

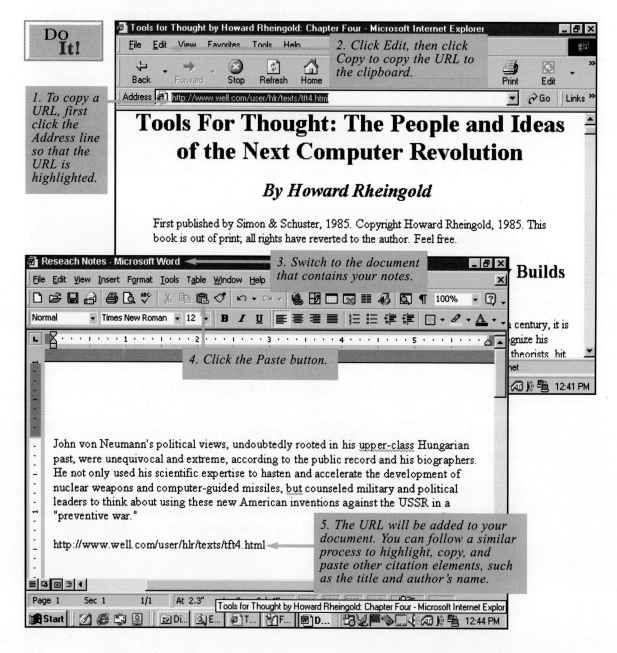

■ To find the date that a Web page was created or last updated, look at the bottom of the page. If the page is not dated, you might find a date on the main page for the Web site.

QuickCheck A

1. True or false? A keyword search for "Ford" is likely to return more results than a search for "Ford automobile". [_____]

2. The plus sign (+) is the symbol for the Boolean operator [_____].

3. If you save a Web page as a [_____] text file, your browser will remove all of the embedded HTML tags.

4. True or false? Each "page" of a Web page corresponds to one printed page. [_____]

5. The *MLA Style Manual* provides details on the format and punctuation for a Web page [_____].

Check It!

QuickCheck B

Indicate the letter that best matches the following:

1. Keyword search [____]

2. Category list [____]

3. Portal site [____]

4. Driving directions [____]

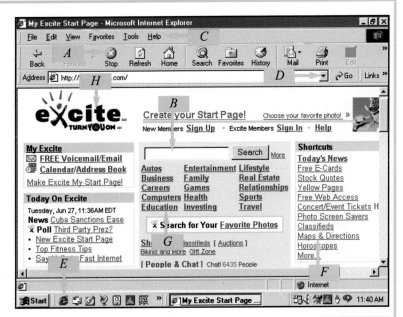

Check It!

Get It?

 **A** Skill Set A: Searching the Web

B Skill Set B: Printing and Saving Web Pages

C Skill Set C: Finding People and Places

D Skill Set D: Copying Text and Graphics

Chapter 5

E-mail Basics

What's Inside?

E-mail can refer to an electronic message or to the entire system of computers and software that handles electronic mail. **E-mail messages** are electronic documents transmitted from one computer to another, usually over the Internet. An **e-mail system** is the equipment and software that carries and manipulates e-mail messages. It includes Internet computers called **e-mail servers** that sort, store, and route mail. An e-mail system also encompasses the personal computers that belong to individuals who send and receive e-mail.

E-mail is an extremely fast method of communication. Most messages are delivered within minutes. E-mail is also essentially free. Once you have a computer with Internet access, you don't pay to send or receive e-mail—no matter how many messages you send, how long the messages are, or where you send the messages.

You use your computer and **e-mail client software** (also called an "e-mail program") to read, compose, and send e-mail messages. In this chapter, you'll learn about four of the most popular e-mail clients: Microsoft Outlook Express, Microsoft Outlook, AOL Mail, and Hotmail.

■FAQ What do I need to send and receive e-mail?

To send and receive e-mail, you need an Internet connection, e-mail client software, and an e-mail account. As you learned in earlier chapters of this book, subscribing to an ISP (Internet Service Provider) provides you with an Internet connection. Your ISP typically also plays the role of postmaster, sets up your e-mail account, and provides you with e-mail client software. You can also obtain an e-mail account from a **Web-based e-mail provider**, such as Hotmail.

Once you've been allocated an **e-mail account**, your e-mail provider can store and deliver your e-mail messages. Your e-mail account has a unique **e-mail address**, which typically consists of a user ID, followed by the @ sign and the name of the e-mail server that manages your electronic post office box. For example, the e-mail address john_smith@mtc.com refers to the e-mail account for John Smith on the e-mail server named mtc.com.

Some ISPs, such as AOL, provide you with special **proprietary e-mail client software** that you are required to install on your computer and use for composing, reading, and sending e-mail. Other ISPs allow you to use the e-mail client of your choice, such as Microsoft Outlook Express, which is included as part of the Windows operating system. You might also be able to use e-mail client software that resides on the Internet, instead of on your computer. The e-mail software that you'll use with Hotmail and other Web-based e-mail providers usually appears as a series of Web pages that you access from the Internet by using your Web browser.

Most e-mail software allows you to compose, send, and receive e-mail in a standard Internet mail format. Because of this standard, you can exchange e-mail messages with virtually anyone who has an e-mail address, even if he or she uses different e-mail software or subscribes to a different ISP.

E-mail is an example of **store-and-forward technology**. When someone sends you a message, it travels over the Internet to your e-mail server (the computer named after the @ sign in your e-mail address). The message is *stored* on the e-mail server until you connect to the Internet and use your e-mail client software to ask for your mail. New messages are then *forwarded*, or transferred, from the e-mail server to your computer. Your e-mail client software puts these new messages in a folder, usually referred to as your **Inbox**. Because your e-mail is stored on the e-mail server until the next time you connect and ask for your mail, you don't have to worry about "missing" an e-mail message when you're not connected. However, some e-mail servers limit the number of messages that they will store for you. Therefore, it is a good idea to check your e-mail regularly—typically one or more times each day—and delete unwanted messages.

■ When you register for an e-mail account, you might be required to select a password. Make sure that your password is easy for you to remember, but difficult for other people to guess. Your password should be at least five characters in length and include numbers, as well as letters. Your e-mail provider might provide additional requirements and recommendations about selecting a secure password.

■ ■ ■

■FAQ Which e-mail program should I use?

The e-mail program that you use might depend on what is installed on your computer or what is required by your e-mail provider. Of course, any e-mail program allows you to accomplish basic e-mail tasks, such as composing e-mail messages, reading and replying to messages, storing messages, and deleting messages. Most e-mail software also includes an address book, which allows you to select addresses from a list instead of typing them. You can also expect a spelling checker. Beyond these basic tasks, every e-mail program has some advantages and a few disadvantages. The next pages of this FAQ summarize the pros and cons of Microsoft Outlook Express, Microsoft Outlook, AOL Mail, and Hotmail.

Microsoft **Outlook Express** is an example of basic e-mail client software. While it does not include many extra features, it does provide an easy-to-use interface for sending and receiving e-mail. For most people, Outlook Express is a good choice for e-mail software.

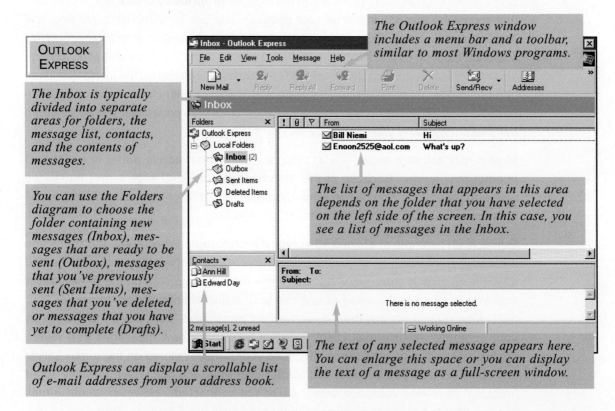

OUTLOOK EXPRESS

The Inbox is typically divided into separate areas for folders, the message list, contacts, and the contents of messages.

You can use the Folders diagram to choose the folder containing new messages (Inbox), messages that are ready to be sent (Outbox), messages that you've previously sent (Sent Items), messages that you've deleted, or messages that you have yet to complete (Drafts).

Outlook Express can display a scrollable list of e-mail addresses from your address book.

The Outlook Express window includes a menu bar and a toolbar, similar to most Windows programs.

The list of messages that appears in this area depends on the folder that you have selected on the left side of the screen. In this case, you see a list of messages in the Inbox.

The text of any selected message appears here. You can enlarge this space or you can display the text of a message as a full-screen window.

■ Outlook Express is included free with most versions of Windows, and is probably already installed on your computer. To see if you have Outlook Express on your computer, click Start, point to Programs, then look for Outlook Express on the Programs menu.

■ Outlook Express can be configured to work with most e-mail providers except those that require proprietary e-mail software, such as AOL.

■ Outlook Express can handle multiple e-mail accounts for a single person. However, it is difficult to set up unique e-mail accounts for multiple people who use the same computer.

■ ■ ■

■ Which e-mail program should I use? (continued)

Microsoft **Outlook** is the deluxe version of Outlook Express. The interfaces of the two programs have many similarities, so it is easy to learn how to use Outlook, if you decide to upgrade. Outlook includes most of the features of Outlook Express, but integrates your e-mail with a To Do list, calendar, contacts list, and personal scheduling. With these extra features, Microsoft Outlook is sometimes referred to as a desktop information management program or a personal information manager (PIM).

Outlook is a good choice if you want tight integration between your e-mail, contacts list, and calendar—for example, if you want to send e-mail from your calendar or search for messages related to an event in your appointment book.

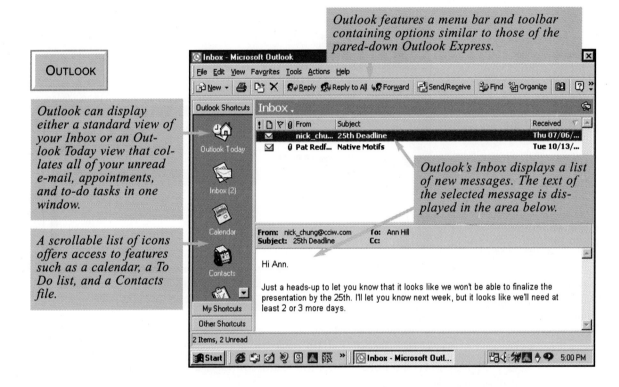

Outlook features a menu bar and toolbar containing options similar to those of the pared-down Outlook Express.

OUTLOOK

Outlook can display either a standard view of your Inbox or an Outlook Today view that collates all of your unread e-mail, appointments, and to-do tasks in one window.

A scrollable list of icons offers access to features such as a calendar, a To Do list, and a Contacts file.

Outlook's Inbox displays a list of new messages. The text of the selected message is displayed in the area below.

■ Outlook features advanced e-mail filtering options that automatically sort, file, delete, highlight, forward, or flag incoming mail according to your specifications. For example, all messages from your boss might be flagged as high priority, whereas junk mail is automatically deleted.

■ Outlook is included with most versions of Microsoft Office, so it might already be installed on your computer system. If you did not receive Outlook with your version of Office, you can purchase it as a separate product from Microsoft. To see if you have Outlook on your computer, click Start, point to Programs, then look for Microsoft Outlook on the Programs menu.

■ Outlook can be configured to work with most e-mail providers except for those that require proprietary e-mail software, such as AOL.

■ Outlook provides a convenient way to back up your e-mail.

■ Which e-mail program should I use? (continued)

AOL Mail is special e-mail client software included as part of the AOL software package. If you subscribe to AOL and have loaded the AOL software on your computer, then you already have the AOL e-mail client and you have an AOL e-mail account. You can use AOL's e-mail client software only if you have an AOL e-mail account.

All AOL e-mail addresses end with @aol.com. Because there are so many users on AOL, most common names, such as john_smith@aol.com, were assigned long ago, leaving current AOL users with e-mail addresses like jsmith223747@aol.com.

Although AOL Mail is a proprietary e-mail system, it can exchange messages with other Internet e-mail systems.

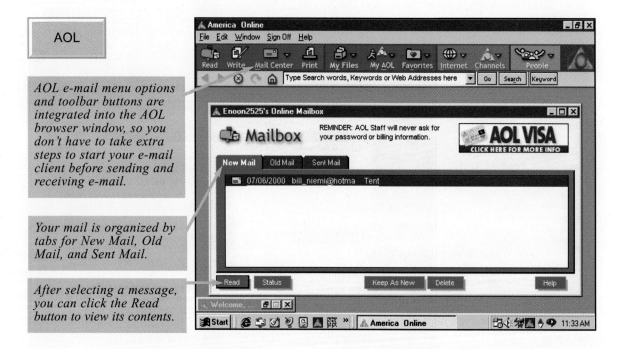

AOL e-mail menu options and toolbar buttons are integrated into the AOL browser window, so you don't have to take extra steps to start your e-mail client before sending and receiving e-mail.

Your mail is organized by tabs for New Mail, Old Mail, and Sent Mail.

After selecting a message, you can click the Read button to view its contents.

■ AOL Mail provides parental control features that are not available on most other e-mail systems.

■ Although AOL Mail was designed to be "user-friendly," in a number of ways it can be more cumbersome to use than more traditional e-mail client software such as Outlook Express. For example, AOL Mail does not automatically show the text of messages to which you are replying, and you must take special steps if you want to read and write messages while you are offline.

■ E-mail attachments are more complex to handle with AOL Mail than with some other e-mail clients. If you work with many attachments, you might want to consider an alternative e-mail provider.

■ Which e-mail program should I use? (continued)

Hotmail is an example of **Web-based e-mail**. To use Hotmail, you don't need to install any special e-mail software on your computer. Instead, you just use any Web browser to go to www.hotmail.com where you can sign in and access your e-mail messages. Hotmail is free and it is accessible from any computer that has an Internet connection. It is an excellent choice for students and for people who travel frequently.

HOTMAIL

Hotmail runs in a browser, such as Internet Explorer.

Your Hotmail Inbox displays a list of both old and new messages. To eliminate old messages from the list, you must delete them.

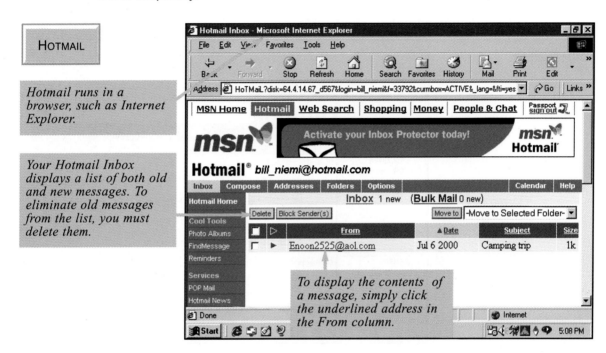

To display the contents of a message, simply click the underlined address in the From column.

■ Hotmail is ideal as a second e-mail account. Even if you have an e-mail account through a university or business, you might want to establish a Hotmail account for your personal e-mail.

■ When you travel, you can configure Hotmail to automatically receive e-mail messages that would otherwise arrive at your business or home computer.

■ Hotmail allows you to automatically direct an arriving message into a specific folder. It can also be configured to block junk mail and messages from specified senders.

■ Because the Hotmail program runs within your browser, you have to be connected to the Internet while you read and write e-mail messages. With other e-mail software such as Outlook and Outlook Express, you can write new messages and read old messages while offline.

■ Mail that is received by your Hotmail account is stored on the Hotmail Internet server, not on your personal computer's hard disk. So, with Hotmail, you're not likely to lose important e-mail if your hard disk crashes. However, your messages are not under your direct control as they would be on your computer's hard disk. You should read the Hotmail privacy policy posted at the Hotmail site.

■FAQ How do I start my e-mail program?

Outlook Express is very easy to start, perhaps because it is so closely integrated with Windows. The easiest way to start Outlook Express is to click the Outlook Express icon, located on the taskbar. You can also start this e-mail software by clicking Outlook Express on the Program menu or by clicking the Outlook Express icon on the desktop.

OUTLOOK EXPRESS

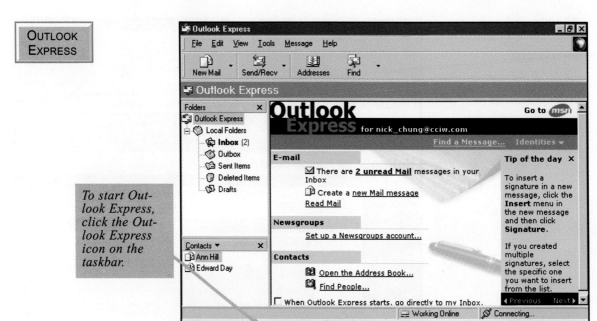

To start Outlook Express, click the Outlook Express icon on the taskbar.

To start Outlook, click Microsoft Outlook on the Programs menu. You might also find a Microsoft Outlook icon on the desktop.

OUTLOOK

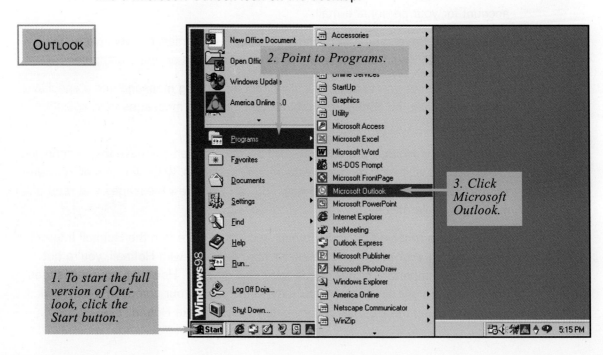

2. Point to Programs.

3. Click Microsoft Outlook.

1. To start the full version of Outlook, click the Start button.

■ How do I start my e-mail program? (continued)

AOL Mail doesn't exist as a separate program. To use AOL Mail, first connect to AOL, then click one of the mail buttons located on the toolbar.

AOL

2. After connecting to AOL, click the Mail Center button, the Read button, or the Write button to access e-mail features.

1. To use AOL Mail, click the AOL icon on the taskbar.

To start Hotmail, first start your browser, such as Internet Explorer or Netscape Navigator. Next, connect to the Hotmail site at www.hotmail.com. Enter your Hotmail user ID and password to sign in to your Hotmail account.

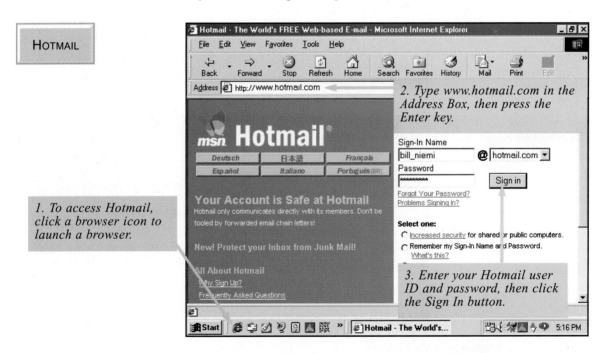

HOTMAIL

2. Type www.hotmail.com in the Address Box, then press the Enter key.

1. To access Hotmail, click a browser icon to launch a browser.

3. Enter your Hotmail user ID and password, then click the Sign In button.

■FAQ How do I write an e-mail message?

In most e-mail programs, you click a toolbar button to start a new e-mail message. Next, you type the e-mail address of the recipient in the To: box. If you want to send a copy of the message to other people, you type their e-mail addresses in the Cc: box. Type a few words to describe the e-mail in the Subject box.

Most e-mail programs provide a sort of mini word processor for writing e-mail messages. You can type your message, edit it, and even check your spelling. Depending upon how your e-mail program is configured, when you click the Send button the message will either be sent immediately or will be placed in the Outgoing mail folder to be sent the next time that you send and receive a batch of messages.

OUTLOOK EXPRESS

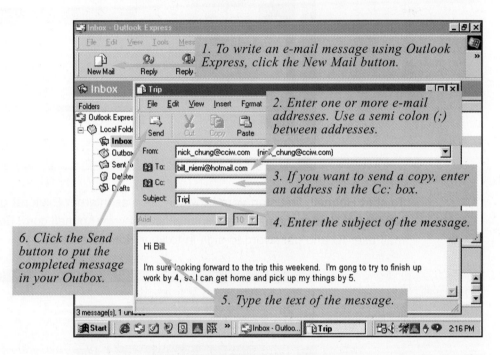

1. To write an e-mail message using Outlook Express, click the New Mail button.

2. Enter one or more e-mail addresses. Use a semi colon (;) between addresses.

3. If you want to send a copy, enter an address in the Cc: box.

4. Enter the subject of the message.

6. Click the Send button to put the completed message in your Outbox.

5. Type the text of the message.

OUTLOOK

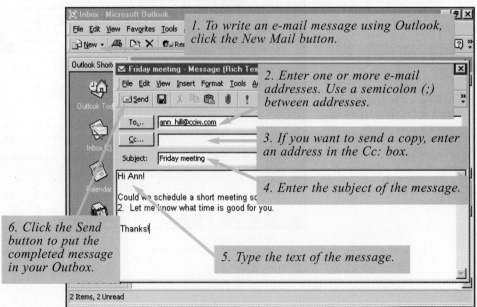

1. To write an e-mail message using Outlook, click the New Mail button.

2. Enter one or more e-mail addresses. Use a semicolon (;) between addresses.

3. If you want to send a copy, enter an address in the Cc: box.

4. Enter the subject of the message.

6. Click the Send button to put the completed message in your Outbox.

5. Type the text of the message.

■ How do I write an e-mail message? (continued)

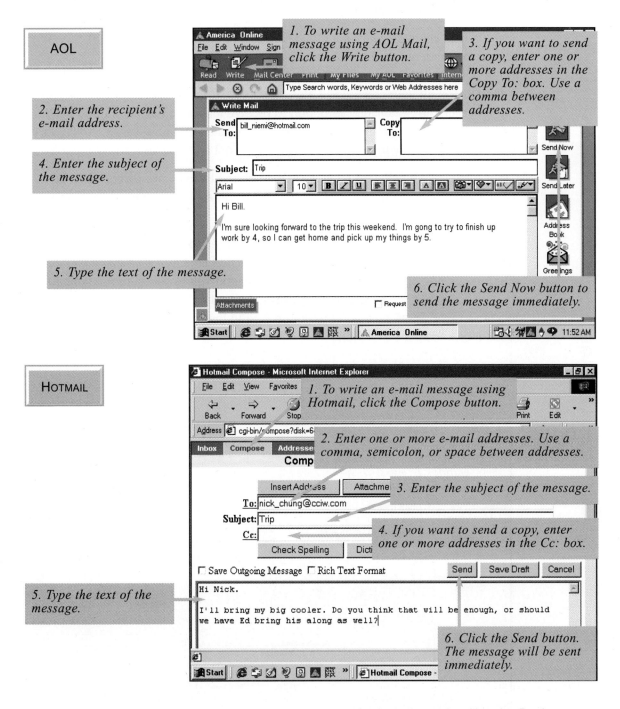

AOL

1. To write an e-mail message using AOL Mail, click the Write button.

2. Enter the recipient's e-mail address.

3. If you want to send a copy, enter one or more addresses in the Copy To: box. Use a comma between addresses.

4. Enter the subject of the message.

5. Type the text of the message.

6. Click the Send Now button to send the message immediately.

HOTMAIL

1. To write an e-mail message using Hotmail, click the Compose button.

2. Enter one or more e-mail addresses. Use a comma, semicolon, or space between addresses.

3. Enter the subject of the message.

4. If you want to send a copy, enter one or more addresses in the Cc: box.

5. Type the text of the message.

6. Click the Send button. The message will be sent immediately.

■ Use the mouse or arrow keys to move the insertion point. Use the Backspace key to delete the character to the left of the insertion point. Use the Delete key to delete characters to the right of the insertion point.

■ As with any word processor, only press the Enter key at the end of a paragraph.

■ Most e-mail programs do not support formatted text, such as bold or italics, unless you are working with mail in HTML format. Both Outlook programs allow you to click Tools, then click Options and use the Send tab to select either plain text or HTML as your mail format.

■FAQ How do I send and receive messages?

Some e-mail client software such as Outlook and Outlook Express are designed so that they can be used to read and write e-mail, even if you are not connected to the Internet. When you click the Send button, the message is temporarily stored in the Outbox on your computer. Later, when you are connected to the Internet, you can click the Send/Receive button to receive incoming messages and send the messages stored in the Outbox. This offline editing feature makes it easy to write, read, and reply to e-mail messages while not tying up your telephone line.

Other e-mail client software such as AOL Mail and Hotmail are designed to be used while you are connected to the Internet. Both AOL and Hotmail messages are sent as soon as you click the Send button.

Outlook Express and Outlook can also be configured to send and receive mail each time that you start the program or at specified time intervals. To configure these programs, click Tools, then click Options and select one of the options from the General tab. This feature is most useful if your Internet connection is always available, as it would be if you are connecting to the Internet through a cable modem or a local area network.

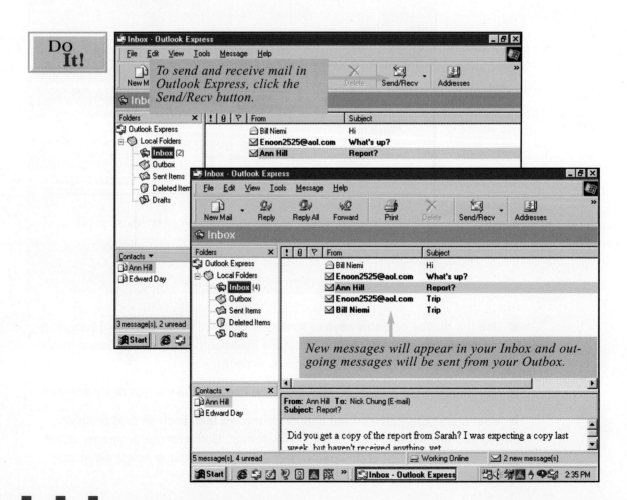

Do It!

To send and receive mail in Outlook Express, click the Send/Recv button.

New messages will appear in your Inbox and outgoing messages will be sent from your Outbox.

■FAQ How do I read and reply to an e-mail message?

When new mail messages arrive in your Inbox, you'll want to read them and perhaps reply to some of them.

To read a message using Outlook Express, double-click the message in the Inbox list. To respond to the message, click the Reply button, then type your response.

OUTLOOK EXPRESS

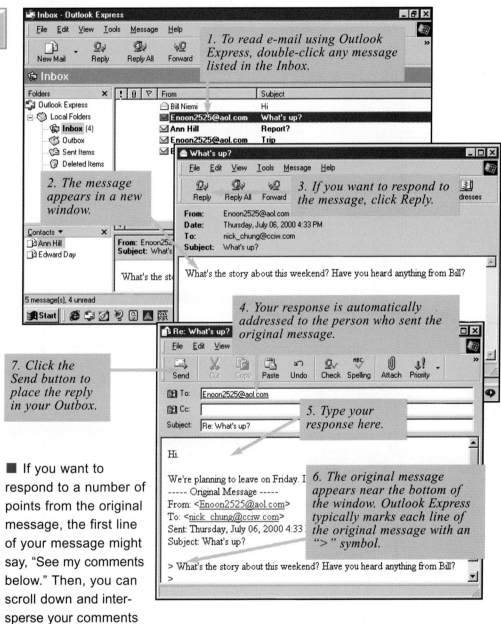

1. To read e-mail using Outlook Express, double-click any message listed in the Inbox.

2. The message appears in a new window.

3. If you want to respond to the message, click Reply.

4. Your response is automatically addressed to the person who sent the original message.

7. Click the Send button to place the reply in your Outbox.

5. Type your response here.

6. The original message appears near the bottom of the window. Outlook Express typically marks each line of the original message with an ">" symbol.

■ If you want to respond to a number of points from the original message, the first line of your message might say, "See my comments below." Then, you can scroll down and intersperse your comments within the text of the original message. To separate your comments from the original message, make sure that your comments do *not* begin with an ">" symbol.

■ If Outlook Express does not display the text of the original message as part of your reply, click the Tools menu, then select Options. Select the Send tab, then make sure that a check mark appears in the box for *Include message in reply*.

■ How do I read and reply to an e-mail message? (continued)

You read and reply to mail in Outlook in much the same way as in Outlook Express. Double-click any message listed in your Inbox to read it. If you want to respond to a message, click the Reply button then type your reply in the space above the original message.

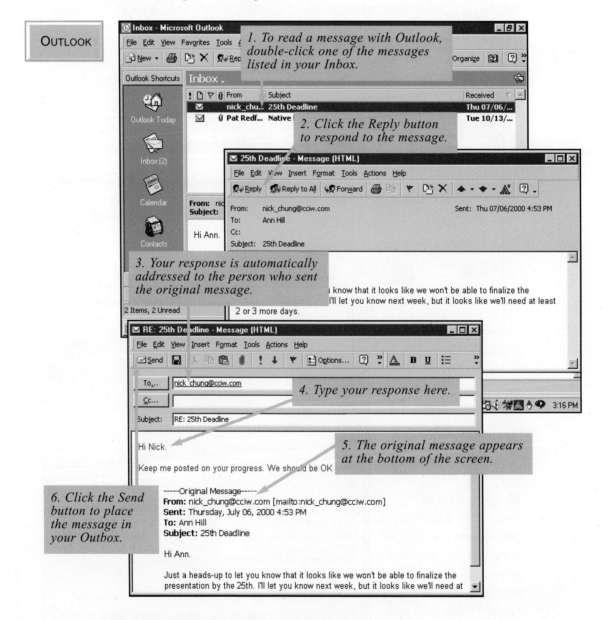

■ If Outlook does not display the text of the original message as part of your reply, click the Tools menu, then select Options. Select the Send tab, then make sure that a check mark appears in the box for *Include message in reply*.

■ If you want to respond to a number of points from the original message, the first line of your message might say, "See my comments below." Then, you can scroll down and intersperse your comments within the text of the original message.

■ How do I read and reply to an e-mail message? (continued)

To read a message using AOL Mail, select the message, then click the Read button. To respond to the message, simply click the Reply button.

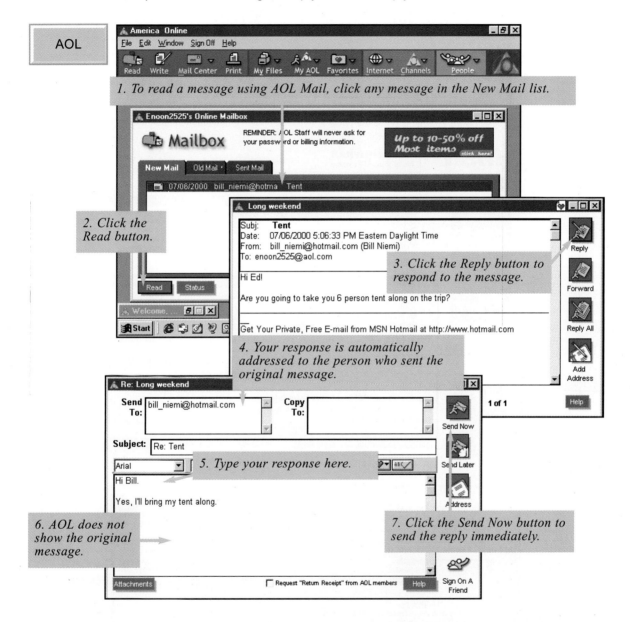

■ Unlike Outlook and Outlook Express, AOL Mail does not show the text of the original message. To add the text of the old message to your response, select the text of the original message, then click the Reply button again.

■ Typically, your reply will be sent as soon as you click the Send Now button.

■ How do I read and reply to an e-mail message? (continued)

To read a message using Hotmail, just click the message that you want to read. Click the Reply button to reply to the message. Type your reply, then click the Send button to immediately send the message on its way.

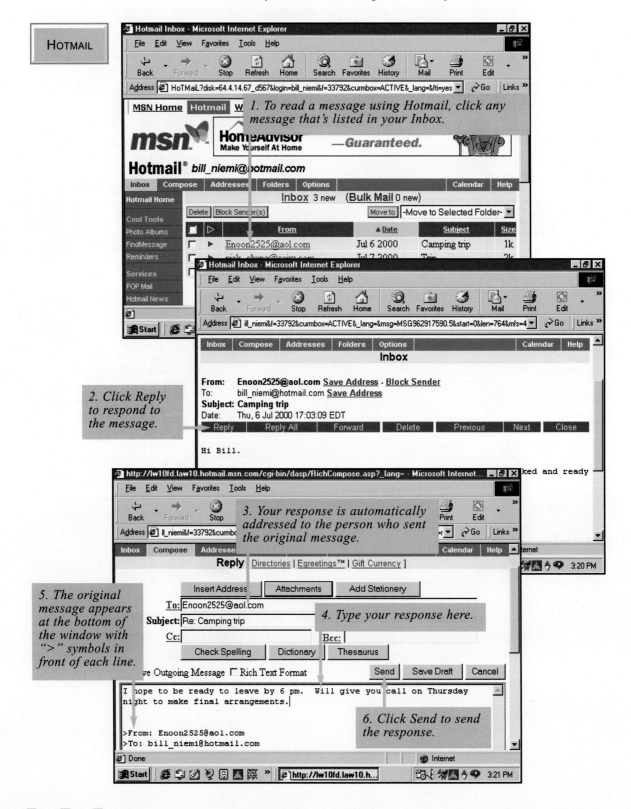

HOTMAIL

1. To read a message using Hotmail, click any message that's listed in your Inbox.

2. Click Reply to respond to the message.

3. Your response is automatically addressed to the person who sent the original message.

4. Type your response here.

5. The original message appears at the bottom of the window with ">" symbols in front of each line.

6. Click Send to send the response.

■FAQ How do I forward an e-mail message?

After you receive an e-mail message, you can pass the message on to other people, a process called **forwarding**. You might use forwarding if you receive a message that should be handled by someone else.

When you initiate the forward, the original message is copied into a new message window, complete with the address of the original sender. You can then enter the address of the person to whom you are forwarding the message. You can also add text to the forwarded message to explain why you are passing it along. Some e-mail software allows you to alter the text of the original message before you forward it. Because a message can be altered before being forwarded, you should be aware that the forwarded messages you receive might not be entirely accurate versions of the original messages.

To forward a message in Outlook Express, click the message, then click the Forward button. Enter the address of the person to whom you want to forward the message, then click the Send button to send the message.

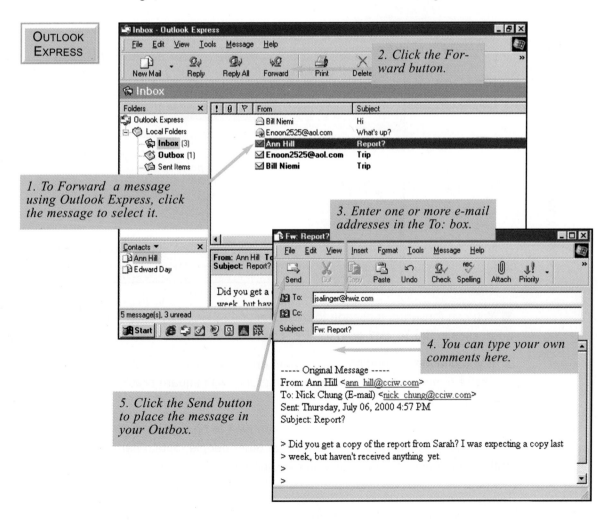

■ How do I forward an e-mail message? (continued)

Forwarding works much the same in Outlook as it does in Outlook Express. Just select the message, click the Forward button, then enter the e-mail address of the person to whom you want to forward the message.

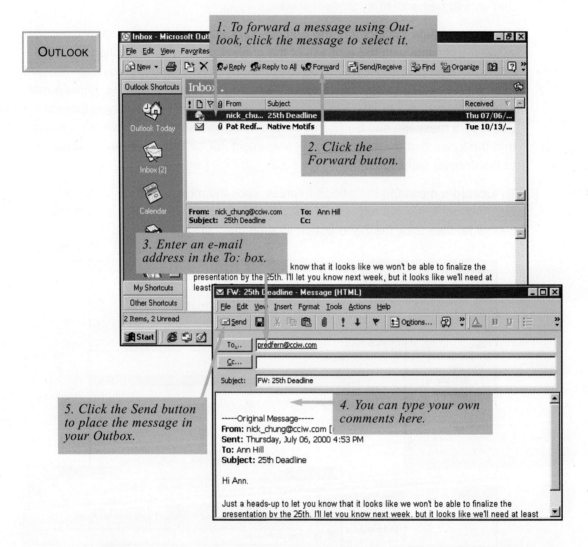

OUTLOOK

1. To forward a message using Out-look, click the message to select it.

2. Click the Forward button.

3. Enter an e-mail address in the To: box.

5. Click the Send button to place the message in your Outbox.

4. You can type your own comments here.

■ You can forward a message to more than one person by entering multiple addresses in the To: box or in the Cc: box.

■ If you change the original message in any way, you should clearly indicate that you have done so by surrounding your material with square brackets and including your initials.

■ Do not forward messages that were intended to be confidential. If you think that such a message needs to be shared with other people, obtain permission from the author of the original message before doing so.

■ How do I forward an e-mail message? (continued)

Forwarding works much the same in AOL Mail as it does in Outlook Express and Outlook. However, AOL Mail does not show the text of the original message, so you can't alter it or refer to it when you type your comments.

AOL

1. To forward a message using AOL Mail, click the message, then click Read.

2. Click the Forward button.

3. Type one or more e-mail addresses in the Send To: box.

4. Click the Send Now button to send the message.

■ How do I forward an e-mail message? (continued)

Forwarding in Hotmail works much the same as in the other e-mail programs. Just open the message, click the Forward button, then enter the e-mail address of the person to whom you want to forward the message.

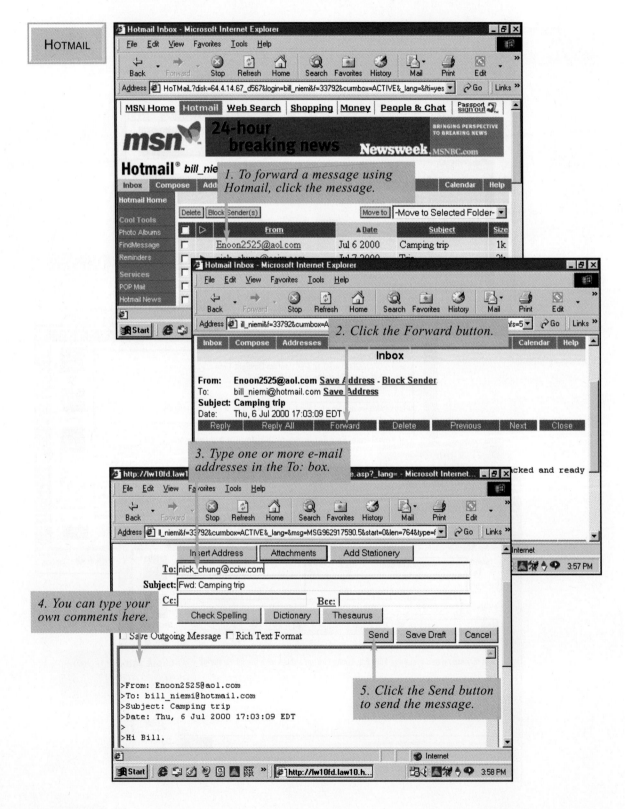

■FAQ How do I delete e-mail messages?

If you save every e-mail message that you receive, your mail will eventually take up a lot of disk space and your Inbox list will contain so many message that it will be difficult to locate important old messages. You should delete unimportant messages right away and periodically go back through your Inbox and delete messages that you no longer need.

OUTLOOK
EXPRESS

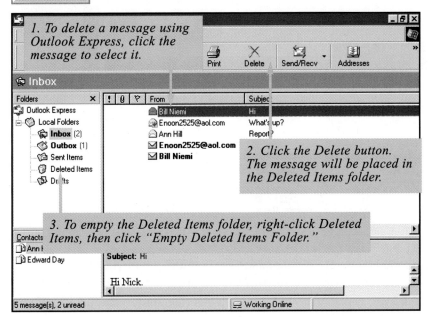

■ You can delete a message while you are viewing it. Simply click the Delete button.

■ In Outlook Express and Outlook, deleted messages are placed in a temporary holding area called the Deleted Items folder. You should periodically empty the Deleted Items folder to permanently remove deleted messages. You can set your e-mail software to automatically empty the Deleted Items folder by clicking the Tools menu, selecting Options, then placing a checkmark in the box for *Empty messages from the Deleted Items folder on exit*.

■ If you mistakenly delete a message, click the Deleted Items folder. Click the message from the Deleted Items list, then use your mouse to drag the message to your Inbox.

OUTLOOK

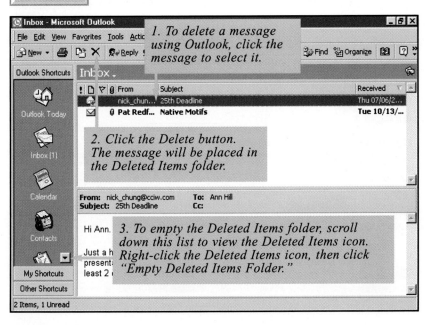

■ How do I delete e-mail messages? (continued)

In AOL Mail, messages that you delete are placed in a Recently Deleted Mail folder. You can access the Mail Center to undelete a message if you act within 24 hours of the time that you made the deletion.

AOL

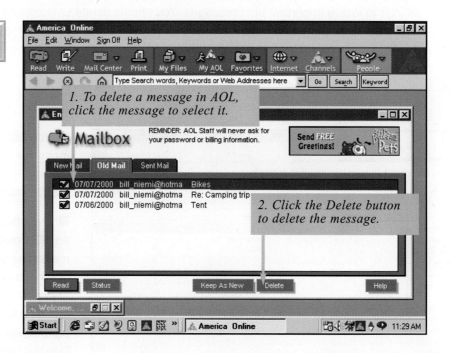

It's important to regularly delete old messages in Hotmail. All of your Hotmail messages are stored on the Hotmail server. You are allocated only a limited amount of space on that server, typically around 2 megabytes (two million characters). If you run out of space, Hotmail won't accept any more mail for your account and you won't receive any new e-mail messages.

HOTMAIL

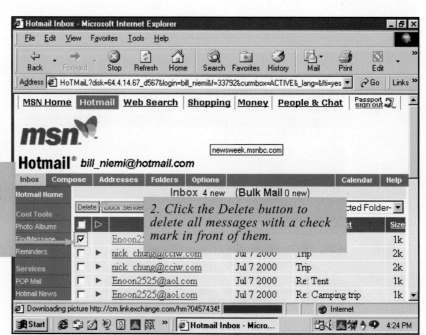

■FAQ How can I create additional e-mail accounts?

If other members of your family want their own mailboxes, they will need their own e-mail addresses. An AOL subscription allows you to create several e-mail addresses, called **screen names**.

If you use Hotmail, you can easily create new e-mail accounts as needed, simply by signing up again as a new user.

If you use Outlook Express or Outlook, you'll typically need to ask your ISP for additional e-mail accounts. Some ISPs allow only one e-mail account for each ISP account—you might be required to purchase new ISP accounts if you want more than one e-mail address. To avoid this expense, you might consider obtaining additional e-mail accounts for free from Hotmail.

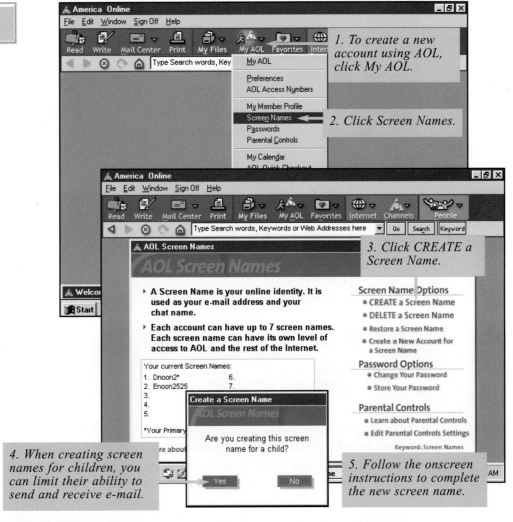

1. To create a new account using AOL, click My AOL.

2. Click Screen Names.

3. Click CREATE a Screen Name.

4. When creating screen names for children, you can limit their ability to send and receive e-mail.

5. Follow the onscreen instructions to complete the new screen name.

■ When this book went to press, AOL supported up to seven screen names for each AOL account. This feature allows every member of most households to have his or her own e-mail account.

■ How can I create additional e-mail accounts? (continued)

Hotmail makes it easy for anyone to create new e-mail accounts as needed. You can create and use Hotmail accounts even though you use Outlook Express, Outlook, or AOL Mail for your main e-mail account.

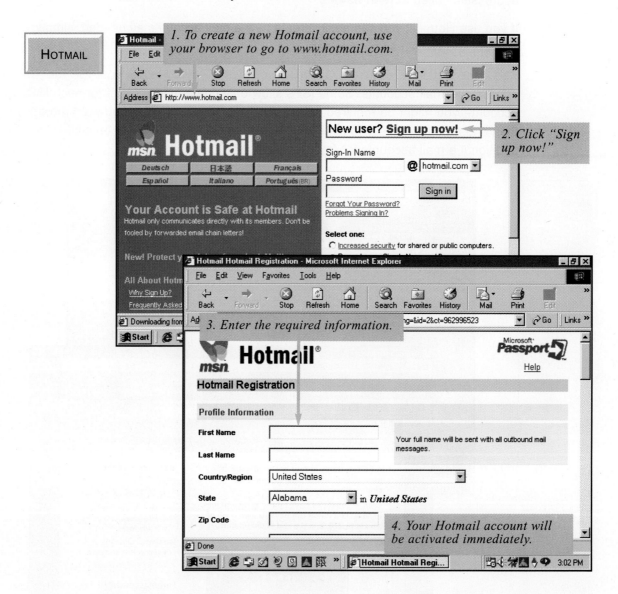

HOTMAIL

1. To create a new Hotmail account, use your browser to go to www.hotmail.com.

2. Click "Sign up now!"

3. Enter the required information.

4. Your Hotmail account will be activated immediately.

■ If you normally use Outlook or Outlook Express, but are using Hotmail to create a second e-mail account to use while you travel, you'll need to tell Hotmail how to get the mail that usually ends up in your Outlook mailbox. To do so, log into your Hotmail account and click the Options button. Select the option for Pop Mail. Fill in the information under the heading "1st Pop Mail Account." You'll find most of the information that you need for this form in your Outlook program by clicking the Tools menu, selecting Options, clicking the Properties button, then selecting the Servers tab. You can click the Hotmail Help button for additional information about completing the Pop Mail Account form.

■FAQ How can I avoid e-mail viruses?

E-mail has become one of the most common ways of "catching" a computer virus because many viruses are distributed as e-mail attachments. Some viruses exist as program files with .exe or .com extensions at the end of the file name. You should never open attachments with these extensions unless you have previously arranged to have someone send you a particular program.

Don't assume that e-mail from your friends is virus-free. Many viruses propagate by stealthily e-mailing themselves to everyone in an address book. Your friends might not even know that virus-infected e-mail is being distributed from their computers.

Prudent e-mail users carefully examine the From and Subject information for each message before opening it. Some document (.doc) and spreadsheet (.xls) files have also been known to harbor viruses. Messages from suspicious sources or with odd attachments should be deleted immediately (and removed from the Deleted Items folder if you are using Outlook or Outlook Express).

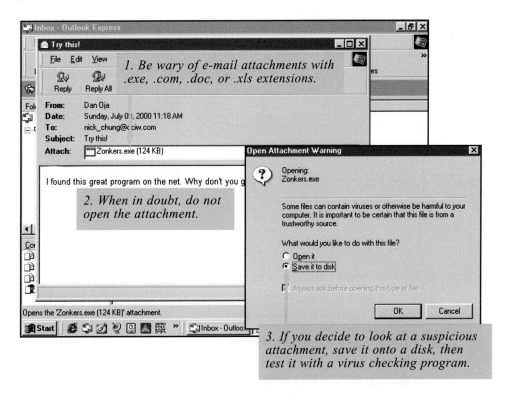

■ If you aren't expecting someone to send you an e-mail attachment, do not open the attachment until you have verified that the sender intended to include the attachment with that e-mail message.

■ For additional protection, install antivirus software on your computer and keep it up to date. Most of this software can be configured to screen your e-mail for viruses before they arrive in your Inbox.

■FAQ How can I back up my e-mail?

As you continue to use e-mail, your address book and archive of old e-mail messages will become more valuable to you. It would be disappointing to lose this information as a result of equipment failure, such as a disk crash.

Only Outlook provides a convenient method for backing up, or archiving, your e-mail and address book. You must use Windows Explorer or any Backup program to back up your files for Outlook Express and AOL Mail. All Hotmail files are stored on the Hotmail server, so there's nothing for you to back up.

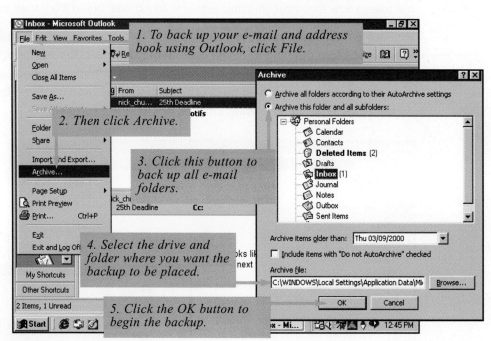

Outlook Express:

■ Use Windows Explorer to back up your Outlook Express address book, which is typically stored in c:\Windows\Application Data\Microsoft\Address Book\xxx.wab where xxx is your e-mail user name.

■ Use Windows Explorer to back up your Outlook Express mail, which is typically stored as a series of .dbx files in c:\Windows\Application Data\Identities\ {23CA0DE0-8C37-11D2-971D-00902717B179}\Microsoft\Outlook Express\. The long number after \Identities\ will vary on each computer.

AOL:

■ Use Windows Explorer to back up the AOL settings and e-mail typically located in c:\Program Files\America Online 4.0\organize\. One file is is named xxxx where xxxx is your screen name. The other file is called xxxx.ARL where xxxx is your screen name.

Hotmail:

■ All Hotmail data is stored on the Hotmail server, so you cannot back up any of those files yourself.

QuickCheck

1. True or false? It usually costs about twice as much to send an e-mail message to another country as it does to send one to a domestic address. [_____]

2. An e-mail [_____] typically consists of a name or nickname, the @ sign, and the name of the computer on which the account is stored.

3. If you use a(n) [_____] e-mail provider, such as Hotmail, you can check your e-mail from any computer that has a browser and Internet access.

4. True or false? When you reply to an e-mail message, the sender's e-mail address is automatically placed in the To: box of the reply message. [_____]

5. Most e-mail viruses have been distributed as [_____] with .exe, .com, .xls, or .doc extensions.

Check It!

QuickCheck B

Indicate the letter of the screen element that you would use to accomplish the following tasks:

1. Forward a message, along with your comments [____]

2. Respond to an e-mail message [____]

3. Remove a message from your Inbox [____]

4. Download new messages [____]

5. Change your e-mail configuration [____]

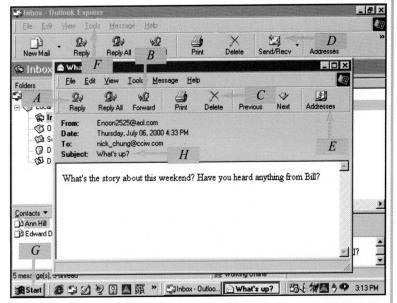

Check It!

Get It?

 Skill Set A: Outlook Express

 Skill Set B: Outlook

C Skill Set C: AOL Mail

D Skill Set D: Hotmail

Chapter 6

E-mail Tips and Tricks

What's Inside?

After you've mastered the basic procedures for composing, sending, and replying to messages, you might want to take advantage of the more advanced features offered by your e-mail software. Some of these features, such as the address book and group addressing, can save you time and can help eliminate typing errors. Other features, such as the use of e-mail attachments and the ability to send and receive e-mail while traveling, can help make e-mail even more useful to you.

■FAQ How do I add names to the address book?

An **address book** is a feature of most e-mail software that allows you to store e-mail addresses, so that you don't have to memorize them. You can add e-mail addresses to your address book in two ways, either manually, by typing in the new address, or automatically, by adding the e-mail address of a person who sends you an e-mail message.

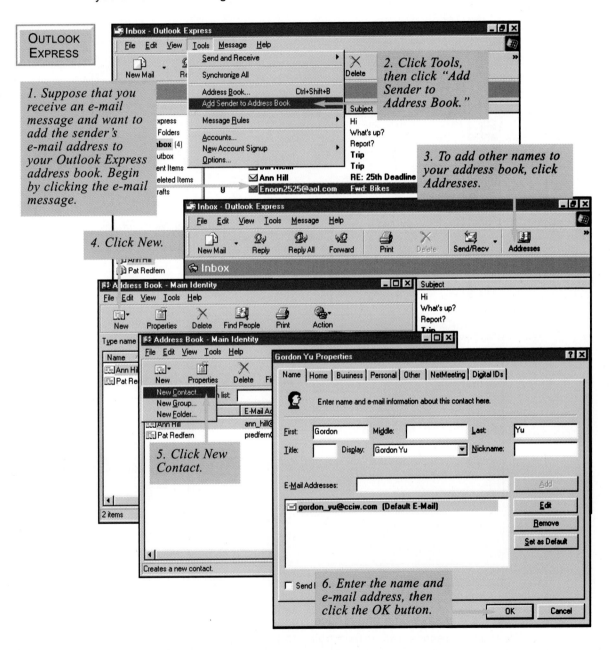

■ You can also add an address by right-clicking the sender's name on the From: line, then clicking *Add to Address Book*.

■ You can use your mouse to highlight an e-mail address in a document or the body of an e-mail message, then copy and paste it into the address book.

■ How do I add names to the address book? (continued)

You can add e-mail addresses to your Outlook address book by using the Tools menu. As an alternative, you can use the right-click method while viewing the list of messages in your Inbox or while viewing the message window.

OUTLOOK

1. To add a name to the Outlook address book, click Tools.

2. Click Address Book.

3. Click the New button.

4. Select New contact.

5. Enter the e-mail address, then click Add button.

■ You can save time and reduce typing mistakes if you copy and paste long e-mail addresses, rather than trying to type them into the address book.

■ The full-featured Outlook address book allows you to store additional information for each contact in your address book, such as home address, business address, phone number, and spouse name.

■ How do I add names to the address book? (continued)

AOL Mail provides a very basic address book into which you can enter a person's first name, last name, and e-mail address. Although space is provided for additional information, don't expect an Outlook-style form laid out with spaces for Home phone, business phone, pager number, address, and so on. Instead, AOL Mail provides a small, free-form Notes box that can accommodate full sentences as well as numbers and addresses.

AOL

1. To add the sender's address from an e-mail that you have received, first open the message, then click the Add Address button.

2. Enter the person's first and last name. AOL Mail should automatically display the e-mail address from the message that you are currently viewing.

3. Optionally, you can enter information, such as a birth date or phone number, in the Notes box.

4. Click OK to save the data.

■ It is not necessary to be viewing an e-mail message in order to add an address to your address book. You can click the Mail Center button, select Address Book, then type in an e-mail address.

■ To delete an address, open the address book, click the name of the person whose address you want to delete, then click the Delete button.

■ How do I add names to the address book? (continued)

Hotmail provides basic address book functions, with one important advantage—because your Hotmail address book is stored on the Hotmail servers, you can access your address book from any computer that has a browser and Internet access. Therefore, your address book is available to you from any computer, anywhere in the world, that you would use to access your Hotmail account.

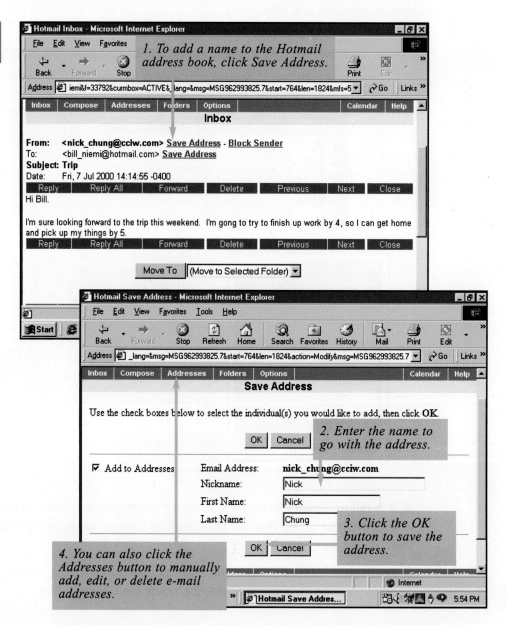

HOTMAIL

1. To add a name to the Hotmail address book, click Save Address.

2. Enter the name to go with the address.

3. Click the OK button to save the address.

4. You can also click the Addresses button to manually add, edit, or delete e-mail addresses.

■ Instead of using the *Save Address* option, you can click the nearby *Block Sender* option to reject all further mail from the person who sent the message.

■FAQ How do I use the address book?

It's much easier to select e-mail addresses from your address book than it is to memorize and type them each time that you send an e-mail message. Your address book will become more useful as you add more names and addresses to it.

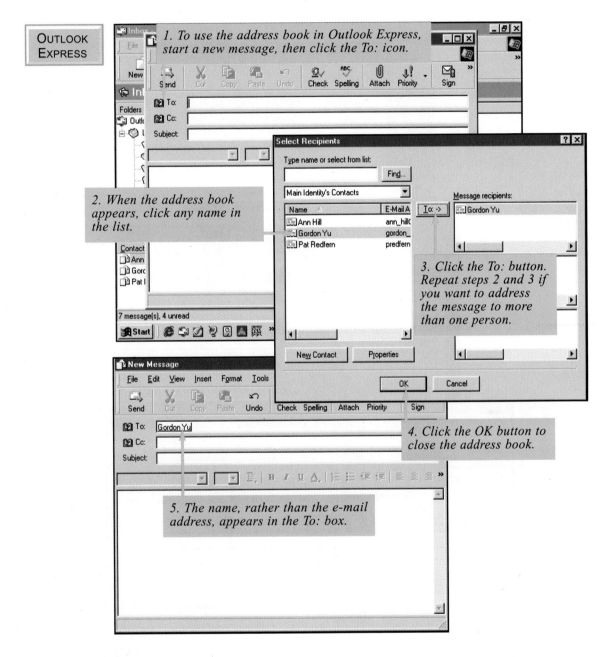

OUTLOOK EXPRESS

1. To use the address book in Outlook Express, start a new message, then click the To: icon.

2. When the address book appears, click any name in the list.

3. Click the To: button. Repeat steps 2 and 3 if you want to address the message to more than one person.

4. Click the OK button to close the address book.

5. The name, rather than the e-mail address, appears in the To: box.

■ When you start to type an address, Outlook Express looks in the address book and tries to complete the address for you. This handy feature means that you only have to type the first few characters of an e-mail address if it is stored in the address book.

■ If you send an e-mail to more than one person, separate the addresses with a semicolon (;).

■ How do I use the address book? (continued)

The address books for Outlook, AOL Mail, and Hotmail work much like the one in Outlook Express. Simply open the address book and select a name from the list to automatically enter the correct e-mail address.

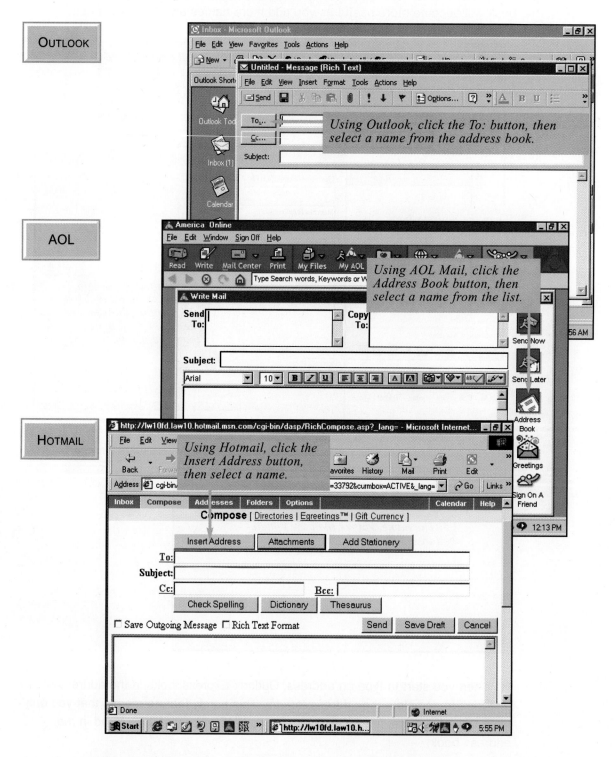

Using Outlook, click the To: button, then select a name from the address book.

Using AOL Mail, click the Address Book button, then select a name from the list.

Using Hotmail, click the Insert Address button, then select a name.

■ As you add more e-mail addresses to your address book, it will become an invaluable reference tool. Make sure that you periodically back up the files containing your address book as explained in the previous chapter of this book.

■**FAQ** How can I send e-mail to many people at the same time?

Sometimes you'll find that you need to send e-mail to a number of people on a regular basis. Rather than entering all of the individual e-mail addresses every time, you can create a **group** in your address book. You might set up a group for your close friends, a committee at work, or the members of your family who have e-mail accounts. When you send an e-mail message to the group, a copy of the message and any attachments are sent to every e-mail address that you've specified for the group.

OUTLOOK
EXPRESS

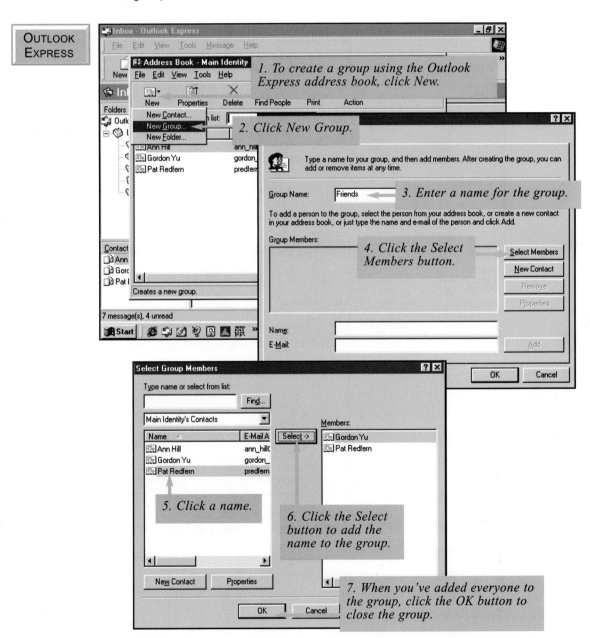

■ To remove a person from a group, open the Outlook Express address book, then double-click the group. Click the name of the person that you want to remove, then click the Remove button.

■ **How can I send e-mail to many people at the same time? (continued)**

Once you've created a group in your Outlook Express address book, you can send mail to the group just as you would send mail to an individual.

OUTLOOK
EXPRESS

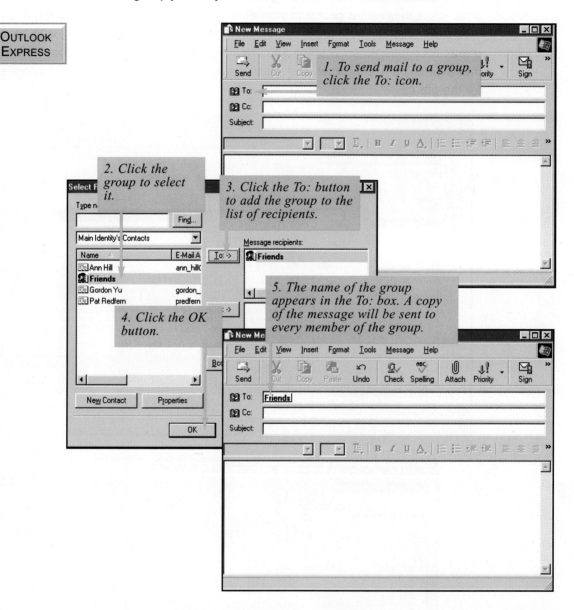

■ Each recipient of the e-mail message will see the e-mail addresses of everyone in the group to which the e-mail was sent.

■ As a shortcut, you can simply start typing the name of the group into the To: box. Outlook Express will search the address book and quickly complete the group name for you.

■ How can I send e-mail to many people at the same time? (continued)

To create a group using Outlook, first you specify a name for the group, then you can select the members of the group from your address book.

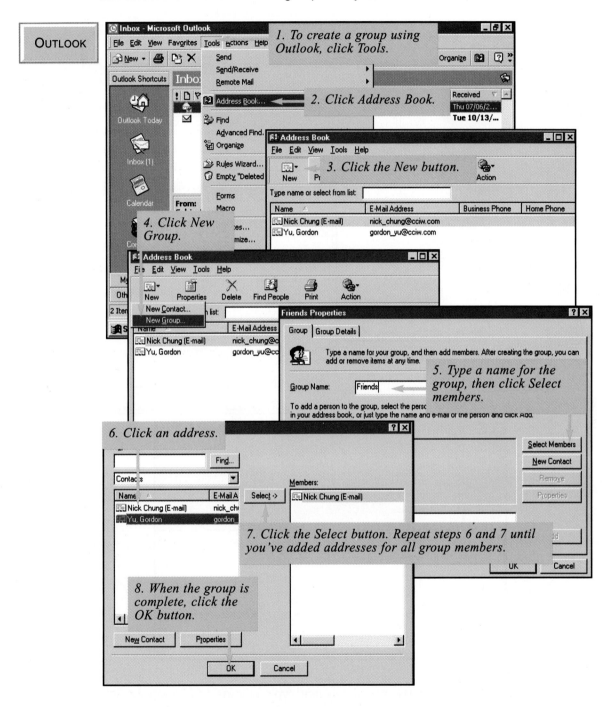

■ How can I send e-mail to many people at the same time? (continued)

To send mail to a group in your Outlook address book, simply select the group from the address book just as you would when sending e-mail to an individual.

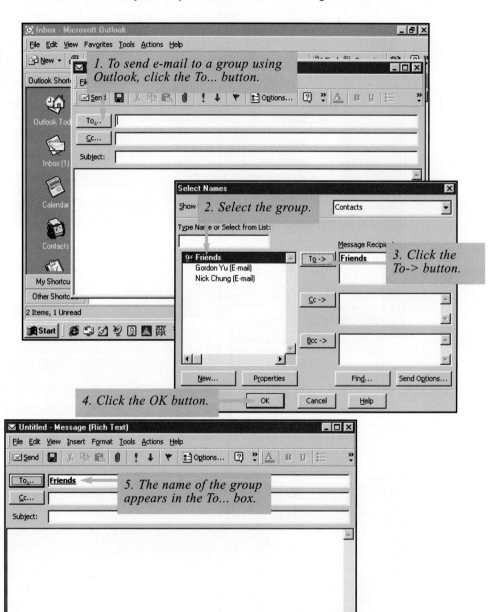

■ As a shortcut, you can simply start typing the name of the group into the To: box. Outlook Express will search the address book and quickly complete the group name for you.

■ Each recipient of the e-mail message will see the e-mail addresses of everyone in the group to which the e-mail was sent.

■ How can I send e-mail to many people at the same time? (continued)

Like other e-mail software, AOL Mail allows you to create groups within your address book. The primary difference is that when you are creating an AOL Mail group you can't select the members of the group from your address book. You must manually type the e-mail address for each member of the group.

AOL

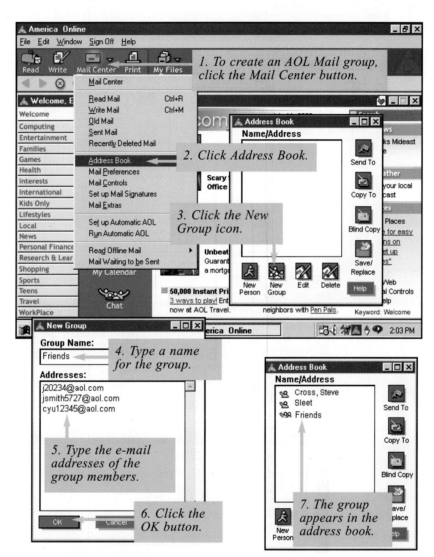

1. To create an AOL Mail group, click the Mail Center button.

2. Click Address Book.

3. Click the New Group icon.

4. Type a name for the group.

5. Type the e-mail addresses of the group members.

6. Click the OK button.

7. The group appears in the address book.

■ Type the e-mail addresses of group members very carefully, then double-check each one to make sure that it is correct.

■ You can send out a test message to the group to check that your addresses are correct. If you've incorrectly typed an address, in most cases you'll receive an "undelivered mail" message indicating an addressing error.

■ You can add addresses to a group by selecting the group, then clicking the address book's Edit button. You can delete a person from a group by using the Backspace key or the Delete key.

■ How can I send e-mail to many people at the same time? (continued)

Sending a message to an AOL Mail group is easy. Simply start a new message, open the address book, and select the group.

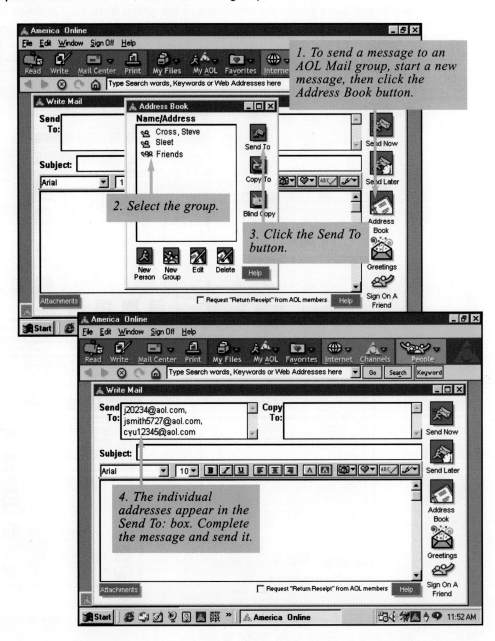

AOL

1. To send a message to an AOL Mail group, start a new message, then click the Address Book button.

2. Select the group.

3. Click the Send To button.

4. The individual addresses appear in the Send To: box. Complete the message and send it.

■ After you've added the group's addresses to the Send To: box, you can delete one or more of the addresses if you don't want to send the message to everyone in the group. This trick would come in handy, for example, if you've defined the addresses for a committee, but want to send a message to a subcommittee.

■ Each recipient of the e-mail message will see the e-mail addresses of everyone in the group to which the e-mail was sent.

■ How can I send e-mail to many people at the same
time? (continued)

When creating a group in Hotmail, you must manually enter the e-mail address of
each member of the group.

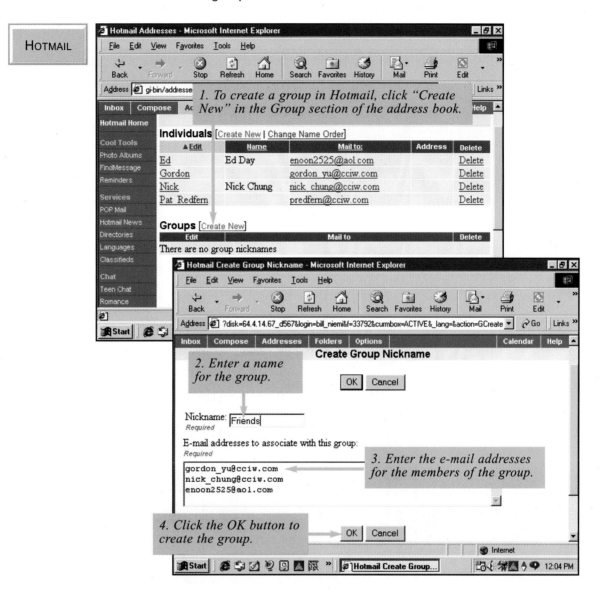

■ Type the e-mail addresses of group members very carefully, then double-check
each one to make sure that it is correct.

■ You can send out a test message to the group to check that your addresses are
correct. If you've incorrectly typed an address, in most cases you'll receive an
"undelivered mail" message indicating an addressing error.

■ To edit or delete an address within a group, click the name of the group where
it appears in the Edit column under the Groups heading.

■ How can I send e-mail to many people at the same time? (continued)

You can send mail to a group in Hotmail the same way that you send mail to an individual. Just place a check mark in front of the group's name to send a copy of the e-mail to every member of the group.

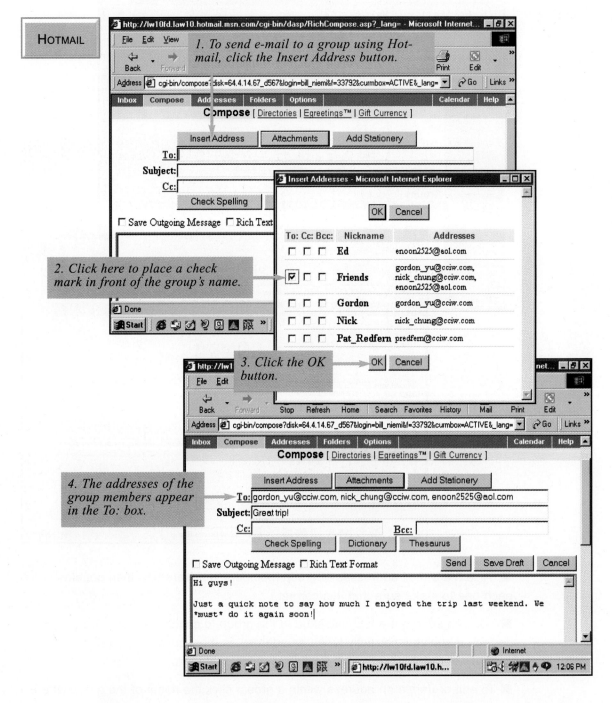

■ As a shortcut, you can simply type the group name in the To: box, instead of accessing the address book.

■ Each recipient of the e-mail message will see the e-mail addresses of everyone in the group to which the e-mail was sent.

■FAQ How do I view and save e-mail attachments?

An e-mail **attachment** is a file such as a document, photo, or worksheet, that is attached to and sent along with an e-mail message. You'll typically want to open and view attachments, such as photos, immediately upon receiving them.

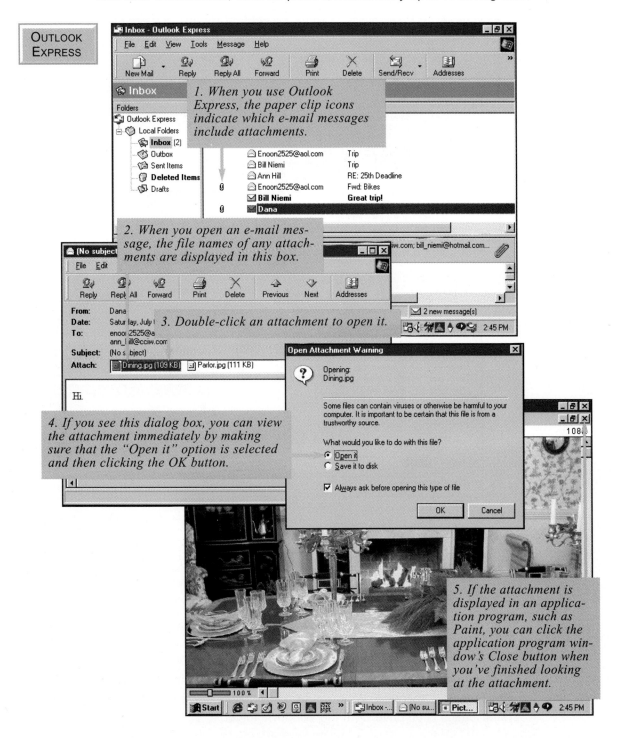

OUTLOOK
EXPRESS

1. When you use Outlook Express, the paper clip icons indicate which e-mail messages include attachments.

2. When you open an e-mail message, the file names of any attachments are displayed in this box.

3. Double-click an attachment to open it.

4. If you see this dialog box, you can view the attachment immediately by making sure that the "Open it" option is selected and then clicking the OK button.

5. If the attachment is displayed in an application program, such as Paint, you can click the application program window's Close button when you've finished looking at the attachment.

■ If you try to open an attachment and see a message asking you to select an application, your computer probably does not have the necessary software. You might have to ask the sender to provide the attachment in a different format.

■ How do I view and save e-mail attachments? (continued)

Sometimes you'll want to save an attachment on your hard disk drive for later use. You might also want to save an attachment so that you can check it with antivirus software before opening it.

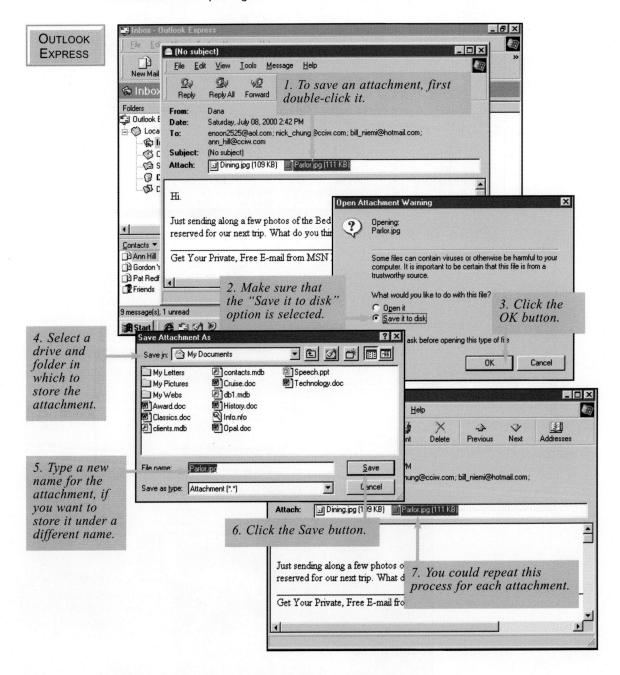

OUTLOOK EXPRESS

1. To save an attachment, first double-click it.

2. Make sure that the "Save it to disk" option is selected.

3. Click the OK button.

4. Select a drive and folder in which to store the attachment.

5. Type a new name for the attachment, if you want to store it under a different name.

6. Click the Save button.

7. You could repeat this process for each attachment.

■ Many people find it helpful to create a special folder in which to store all attachments. Otherwise, Windows typically places these files in a folder called Temp, which is on drive C: in the Windows folder.

■ If your antivirus software is not checking attachments as they arrive, you should save suspicious attachments on your disk before opening them. Once saved, you can use antivirus software to check the files for viruses.

How do I view and save e-mail attachments? (continued)

Outlook handles attachments in much the same way as Outlook Express. You can either open the attachment immediately or save it on your hard disk drive.

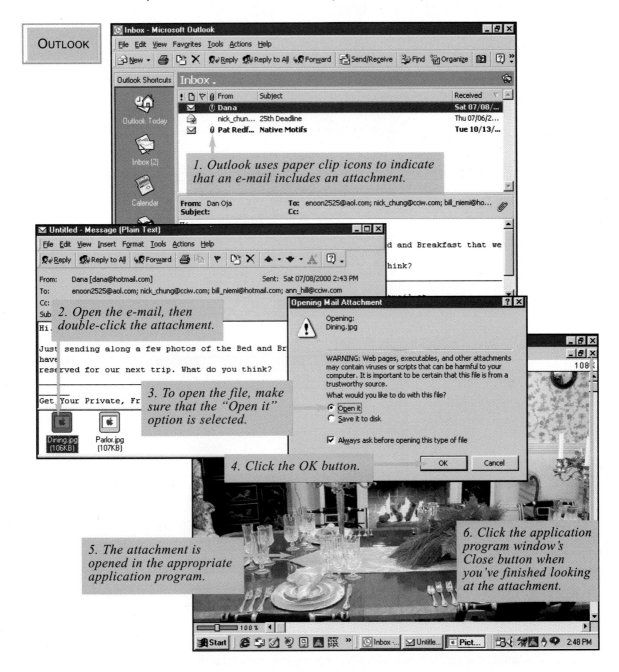

OUTLOOK

1. Outlook uses paper clip icons to indicate that an e-mail includes an attachment.

2. Open the e-mail, then double-click the attachment.

3. To open the file, make sure that the "Open it" option is selected.

4. Click the OK button.

5. The attachment is opened in the appropriate application program.

6. Click the application program window's Close button when you've finished looking at the attachment.

■ If you try to open an attachment and see a message asking you to select an application, your computer probably does not have the necessary software installed to display the attachment. You might have to ask the sender to provide the attachment in a different format.

■ Be particularly careful when opening attachments with .exe, .com, .xls, or .doc extensions because they can contain viruses. You might want to follow the instructions on the next page to save the attachment, then check it with antivirus software.

■ How do I view and save e-mail attachments?
(continued)

Outlook also allows you to save attachments on your hard disk for later use.

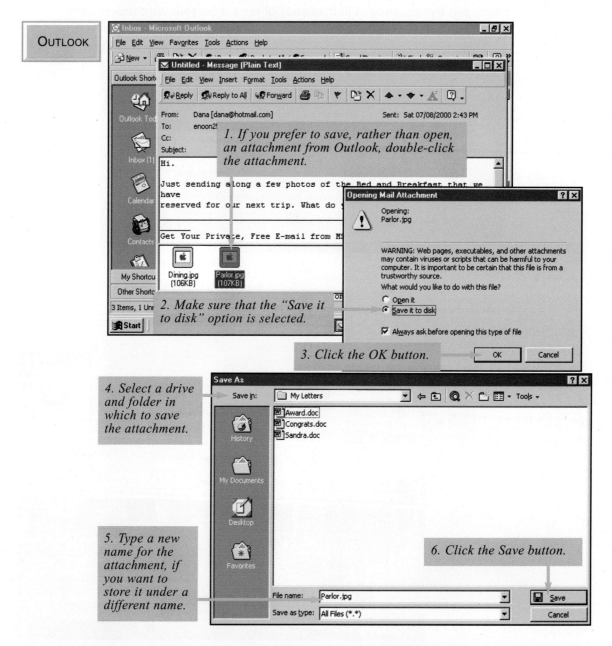

OUTLOOK

1. If you prefer to save, rather than open, an attachment from Outlook, double-click the attachment.

2. Make sure that the "Save it to disk" option is selected.

3. Click the OK button.

4. Select a drive and folder in which to save the attachment.

5. Type a new name for the attachment, if you want to store it under a different name.

6. Click the Save button.

■ Many people find it helpful to create a special folder in which to store all attachments, but you can put them in any folder that helps you to easily locate them later.

■ If you can't find an attachment that you think you've saved, look in a folder called Temp, which is in the Windows folder.

■ How do I view and save e-mail attachments?
(continued)

AOL Mail handles attachments quite differently from Outlook Express and Outlook.
AOL attachments are not transferred from the mail server to your computer until
you click the Download button.

AOL

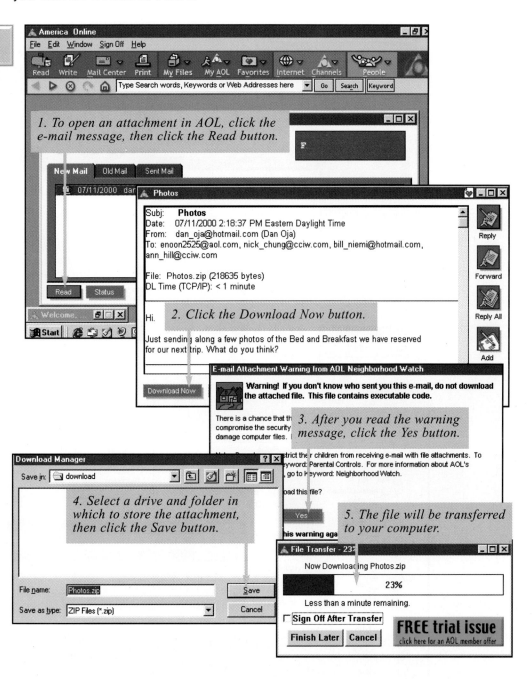

■ Downloaded pictures can be automatically displayed if you've used the Set Programs option on the My AOL button to select the *Display Files on Download*
option.

■ How do I view and save e-mail attachments? (continued)

AOL automatically compresses most attachments. You must decompress an attachment before you can view it with an application program, such as Microsoft Word or Paint.

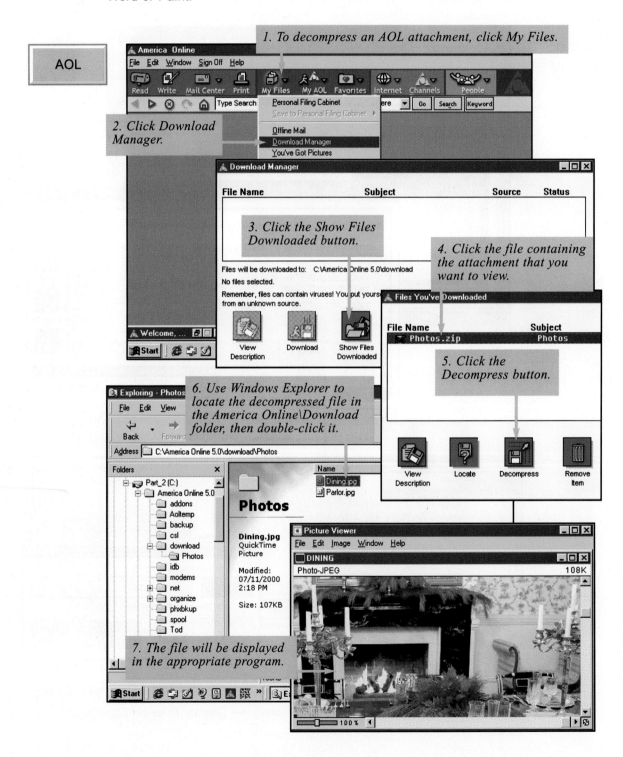

■ How do I view and save e-mail attachments? (continued)

Hotmail automatically displays photo attachments underneath the text of the corresponding e-mail message. Other types of attachments, such as documents, spreadsheets, and sound files must be downloaded before you can view them.

HOTMAIL

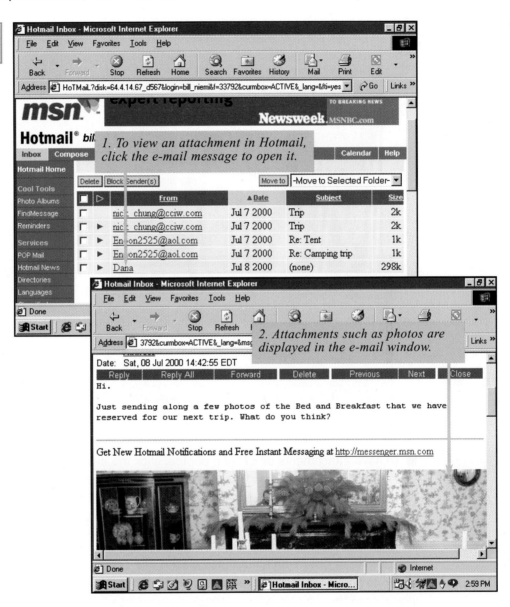

■ If an attachment does not automatically open, click the e-mail message, then click View Attachment. Select the Download File option to open the File Download dialog box. Click the option button for *Open this file from its current location*, then click the OK button.

■ If Hotmail cannot display the attachment automatically, it will display a dialog box that allows you to save the attachment on your computer system. Then you'll need to use an application program to locate and view the attachment.

■ Hotmail automatically checks attachments for viruses before you download them.

■ **How do I view and save e-mail attachments?**
(continued)

Hotmail makes it easy to display and save photos that you receive as e-mail attachments, but it just takes a few additional "clicks" to save other types of attachments.

HOTMAIL

1. *To save a photo attachment that's displayed by Hotmail, right-click anywhere in the picture.*

2. *Click Save Picture As.*

3. *Select a drive and folder in which to save the picture, then click the Save button.*

■ To save attachments other than photos, click the e-mail message, then click View Attachment. Select the Download File option to open the File Download dialog box. Click the option button for *Save file to disk*, then click the OK button. You can then select a drive and folder on your computer as the location for the new file.

■ Some people find it convenient to establish a folder on drive C into which they can download files. With all of these files in one place, it is easy to remember where to find them. It is also easier to work with these files, for example if you'd like to scan them for viruses. In addition, some files that you download will be compressed to make them smaller. You'll need to uncompress them before you can view them. You can keep the compressed version in your download folder, but place the uncompressed version in a project folder, a documents folder, or a music folder with other similar files.

■FAQ How do I send e-mail attachments such as photos?

It's fun to receive and view attachments, but it's also fun to create and send your own attachments to other people. You can attach just about any kind of file to an e-mail message including word processing documents, spreadsheets, photos, and music clips.

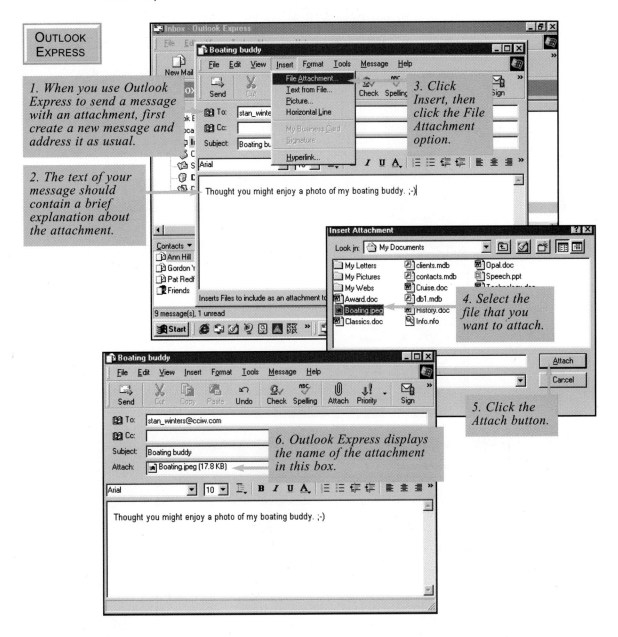

OUTLOOK EXPRESS

1. When you use Outlook Express to send a message with an attachment, first create a new message and address it as usual.

2. The text of your message should contain a brief explanation about the attachment.

3. Click Insert, then click the File Attachment option.

4. Select the file that you want to attach.

5. Click the Attach button.

6. Outlook Express displays the name of the attachment in this box.

■ When you create a file to use as an attachment, it's important to remember what you've called the file and where you've put it so that you can find it when the time comes to attach it.

■ If you're sending large attachments, you might consider compressing them first to reduce transfer time. You'll find more information on compression in the next chapter.

■ How do I send e-mail attachments such as photos? (continued)

When attaching one or more files to an Outlook message, you'll create the message and address it as usual. Use the Insert option from the File menu to open a dialog box that allows you to locate and select the file that you want to attach.

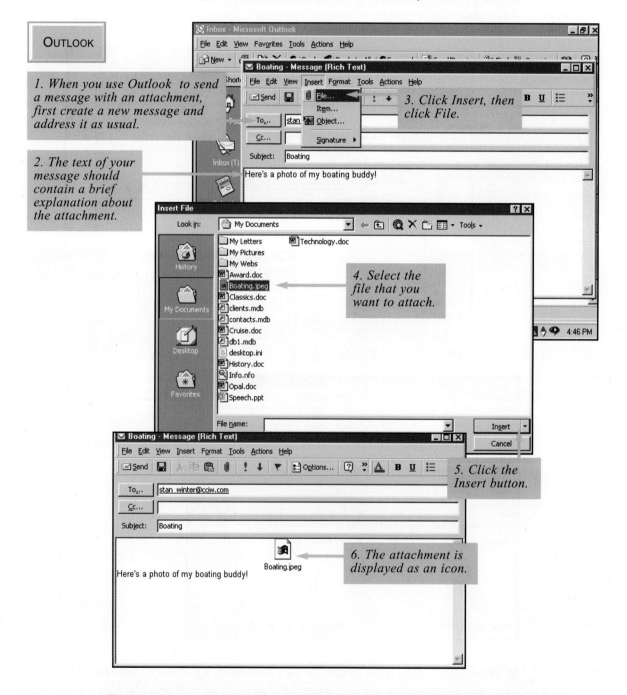

OUTLOOK

1. When you use Outlook to send a message with an attachment, first create a new message and address it as usual.

2. The text of your message should contain a brief explanation about the attachment.

3. Click Insert, then click File.

4. Select the file that you want to attach.

5. Click the Insert button.

6. The attachment is displayed as an icon.

■ When you create a file to use as an attachment, it's important to remember where you put it so that you can find it when it comes time to attach it.

■ If you're sending a large attachment, such as a high resolution photo, you might consider compressing it first to reduce transfer time. You'll find more information on compression in the next chapter.

■ How do I send e-mail attachments such as photos? (continued)

When you create a message with more than one attachment, AOL Mail automatically groups the attachments into a single file and compresses them to save space and minimize transfer time. Your e-mail recipients will have to uncompress the attachments as explained in the next chapter.

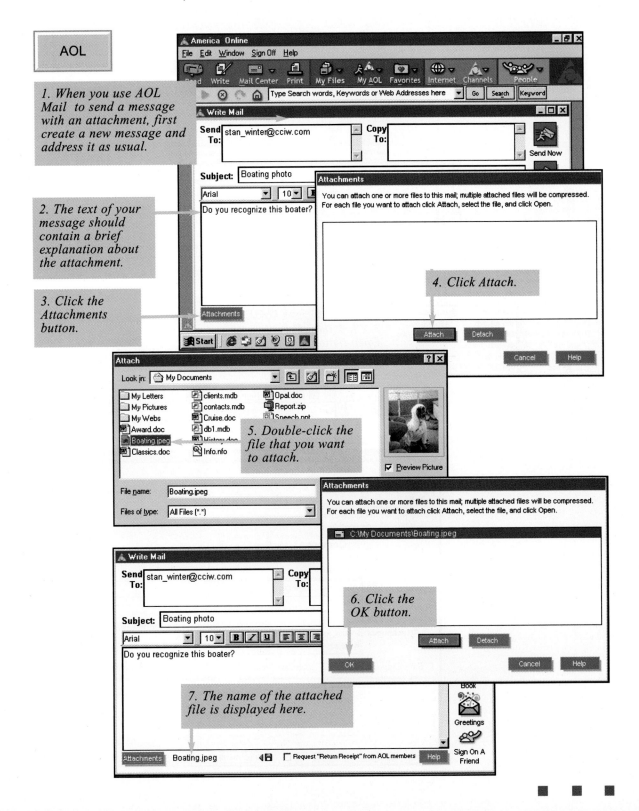

AOL

1. When you use AOL Mail to send a message with an attachment, first create a new message and address it as usual.

2. The text of your message should contain a brief explanation about the attachment.

3. Click the Attachments button.

4. Click Attach.

5. Double-click the file that you want to attach.

6. Click the OK button.

7. The name of the attached file is displayed here.

How do I send e-mail attachments such as photos? (continued)

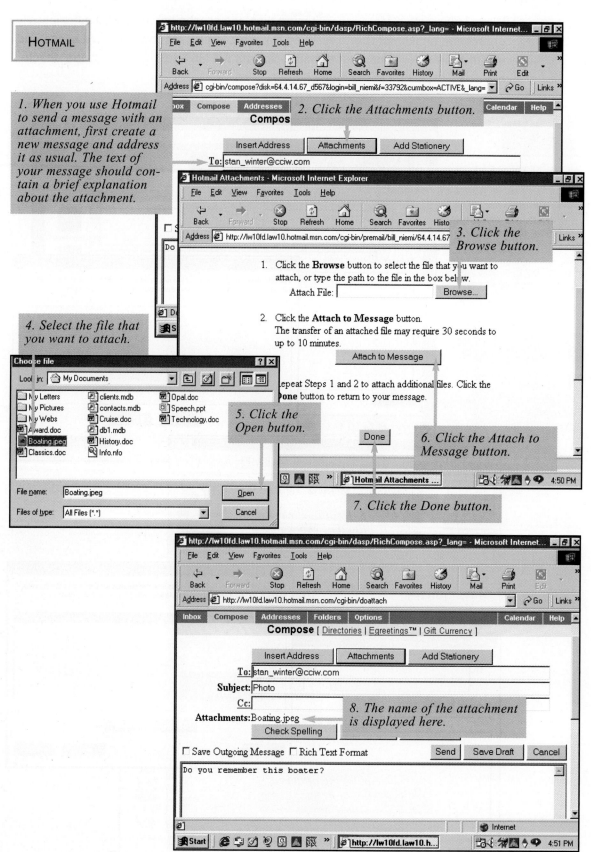

HOTMAIL

1. When you use Hotmail to send a message with an attachment, first create a new message and address it as usual. The text of your message should contain a brief explanation about the attachment.

2. Click the Attachments button.

3. Click the Browse button.

4. Select the file that you want to attach.

5. Click the Open button.

6. Click the Attach to Message button.

7. Click the Done button.

8. The name of the attachment is displayed here.

■FAQ How can I get my e-mail while traveling?

AOL and Hotmail users can easily reach their e-mail from any computer that has a browser and Internet access. Outlook Express and Outlook users often find that the easiest way to reach their e-mail while traveling is to set up a special Hotmail account for use while on the road, as explained later in this chapter.

AOL maintains a special Web site called AOL.com, that allows AOL users to access their e-mail from any computer that has Internet access. Instead of using your locally installed and personalized AOL e-mail client software, AOL.com uses a Web-based e-mail client that displays your mail from any Web browser.

AOL

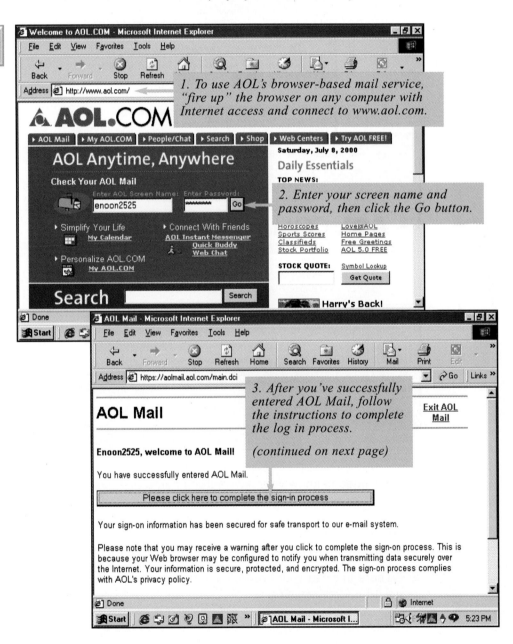

1. To use AOL's browser-based mail service, "fire up" the browser on any computer with Internet access and connect to www.aol.com.

2. Enter your screen name and password, then click the Go button.

3. After you've successfully entered AOL Mail, follow the instructions to complete the log in process.

(continued on next page)

■ How can I get my e-mail while traveling?
(continued)

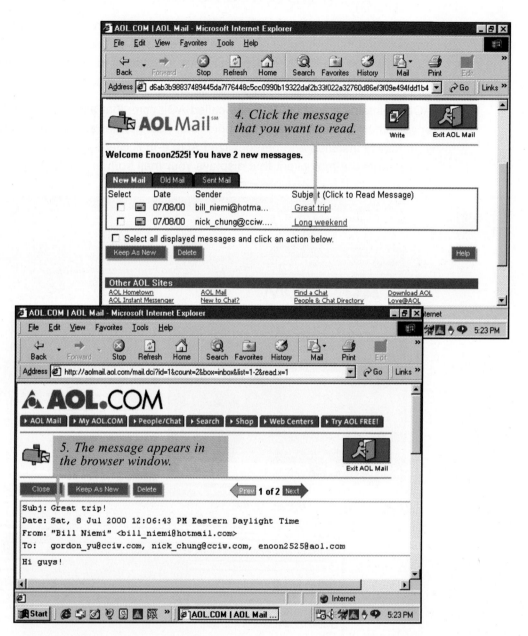

■ You'll need to know your AOL screen name and password in order to access your AOL account through a browser.

■ Your AOL address book is not available when using AOL.com, so you should take a list of e-mail addresses with you when you travel.

■ Be sure to close your browser when you're finished, so that no one else can use your e-mail account.

■ How can I get my e-mail while traveling? (continued)

As you've already learned, Hotmail is a Web-based e-mail provider that displays your mail from within a browser. You can easily access your Hotmail account from any computer that has an Internet connection and a browser. As a result, Hotmail is one of the most travel-friendly e-mail providers.

HOTMAIL

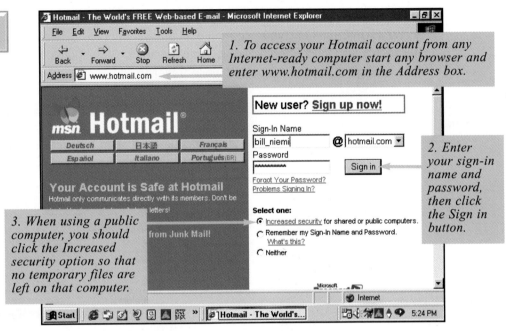

1. To access your Hotmail account from any Internet-ready computer start any browser and enter www.hotmail.com in the Address box.

2. Enter your sign-in name and password, then click the Sign in button.

3. When using a public computer, you should click the Increased security option so that no temporary files are left on that computer.

■ Make sure that you close the browser when you're finished, so that no one else can use your e-mail account.

■ Because your Hotmail address book is stored on the e-mail server, you can use your address book from any computer on the Internet.

■ When you use Hotmail on your home computer, you can configure it to automatically enter your password. When using a public computer, however, you'll have to enter your sign-in name and password each time that you use Hotmail. Therefore, you should memorize your sign-in name and password before you "hit the road."

■ How can I get my e-mail while traveling? (continued)

If you use Outlook or Outlook Express and have an ISP as your e-mail provider, you probably have what's called a **POP account**. POP, which stands for "Post Office Protocol," is the technology that your ISP's e-mail server uses to store and deliver your mail. You can configure Hotmail to check messages stored in your POP mail account. If you do so, when you travel, you can use Hotmail to access any new mail that arrives either in your Hotmail account or in your POP mail account. Unfortunately, your Hotmail account will not provide access to old mail stored in your Outlook Inbox, so you might want to print copies of any important old message that you might need while traveling.

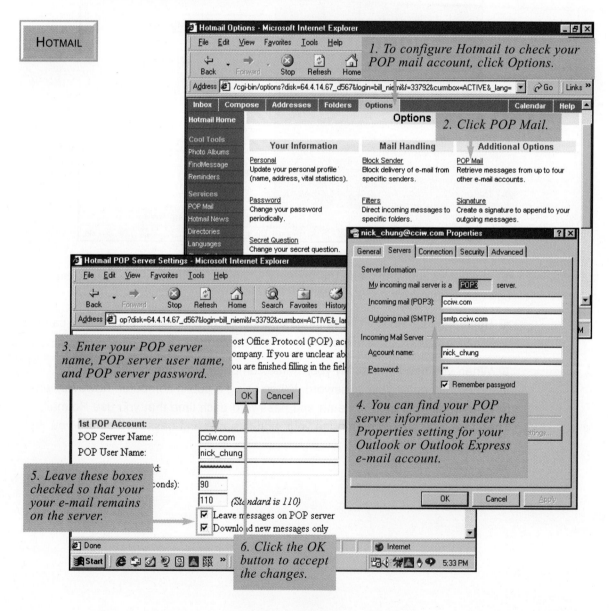

HOTMAIL

1. To configure Hotmail to check your POP mail account, click Options.

2. Click POP Mail.

3. Enter your POP server name, POP server user name, and POP server password.

4. You can find your POP server information under the Properties setting for your Outlook or Outlook Express e-mail account.

5. Leave these boxes checked so that your your e-mail remains on the server.

6. Click the OK button to accept the changes.

■ If you don't want to configure Hotmail to get mail from your POP account, simply give your Hotmail e-mail address to anyone who might need to contact you while you're traveling. If you do so, however, you might still have a number of important messages stacking up on your POP account while you are away.

QuickCheck A

1. A(n) [_____] is a feature of e-mail software that allows you to store e-mail addresses so that you don't have to memorize them.

2. True or false? You can reach your Hotmail address book from any computer that has a browser and an Internet connection. [_____]

3. When you send e-mail to a(n) [_____], a copy of the e-mail message will be sent to everyone who is a member of it.

4. When you receive an e-mail message with an attachment, you can either open the attachment or [_____] it on your computer system for later use.

5. True or false? Outlook Express and Outlook make it easy to access your e-mail while traveling. [_____]

Check It!

QuickCheck B

Indicate the letter of the screen element that best matches the following:

2. An individual e-mail address [___]

2. An e-mail group [___]

3. The button you click to add a name to the address book [___]

4. The button you click to select a name from the address book [___]

5. The destination address for this e-mail [___]

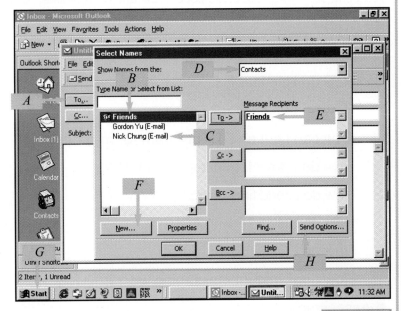

Check It!

Get It?

 Skill Set A: Outlook Express

B Skill Set B: Outlook

C Skill Set C: AOL Mail

D Skill Set D: Hotmail

Chapter 7
Zip, FTP, and Chat

What's Inside?

In previous chapters you learned how to send and receive files as e-mail attachments. Many of the files that zoom over the Internet as attachments are quite large, and they can take some time to download from an e-mail server to the recipient's computer. It is, therefore, considered polite to reduce the size of large files before sending them as attachments. In this chapter you'll learn how to use WinZip, a popular compression utility, to compress large files so that you can send them over the Internet more quickly.

Even with compression, however, some files or groups of files are really too large to send as attachments. For transmitting and receiving very large files, an Internet utility called FTP might be preferable to attachments. In this chapter, you'll learn how to use an FTP program to upload and download files over the Internet.

The conclusion of this chapter on handy Internet utilities looks at chat and instant messaging. You'll find out how to use these popular instant, or "real time," communications tools.

■ FAQs:

■FAQ How can I get a Zip program for my computer?

A "Zip program" is the popular term for compression software that that allows you to reduce the size of one or more files, without losing any of their contents. Because a file that has been zipped is smaller than the original, it requires less storage space and can be transmitted over the Internet much more quickly than the original file.

WinZip is one of the most popular Zip programs available today. You can download and install a free, evaluation-version of this program. If you decide to use it on a regular basis, you can obtain the registered version using a credit card.

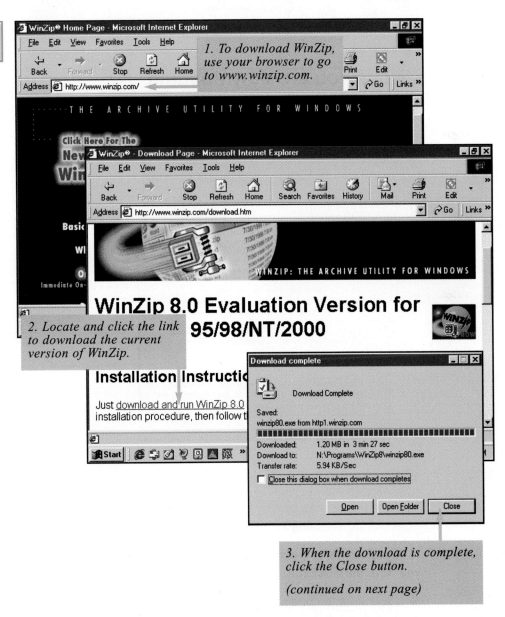

1. To download WinZip, use your browser to go to www.winzip.com.

2. Locate and click the link to download the current version of WinZip.

3. When the download is complete, click the Close button.

(continued on next page)

■ **How can I get a Zip program for my computer?
(continued)**

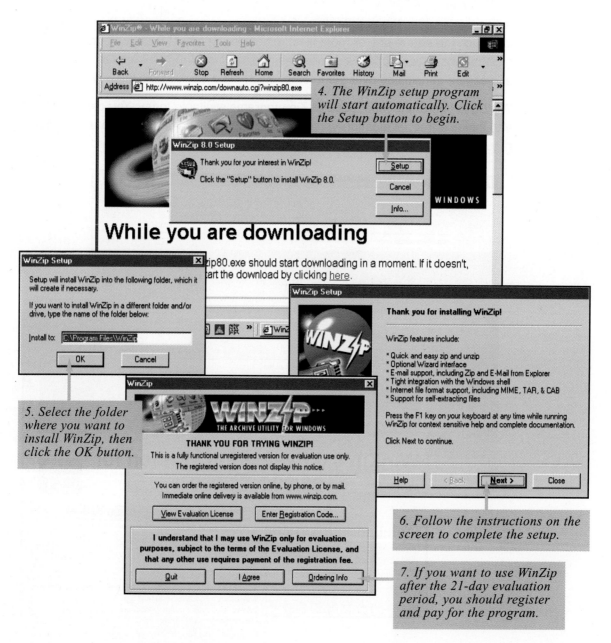

■ Once WinZip has been installed, you can access it by clicking the Windows Start button, selecting Programs, then selecting the WinZip option.

■ If you are using a school lab computer or a computer at work, make sure that you have permission to download and install files before you try to get WinZip.

■ If you want to continue using WinZip after the free trial period, you should click the Ordering Info button on the WinZip dialog box to find out how to pay for and register your copy of WinZip.

■FAQ How do I zip files?

You can zip a single file to reduce its size. You can also zip multiple files, creating a single file that is smaller than the combined size of the original files. If you're planning to, for example, send several files along with an e-mail message, you might consider zipping all of them into a single file. Then you'll go through the attachment procedure for only one file instead of for many files.

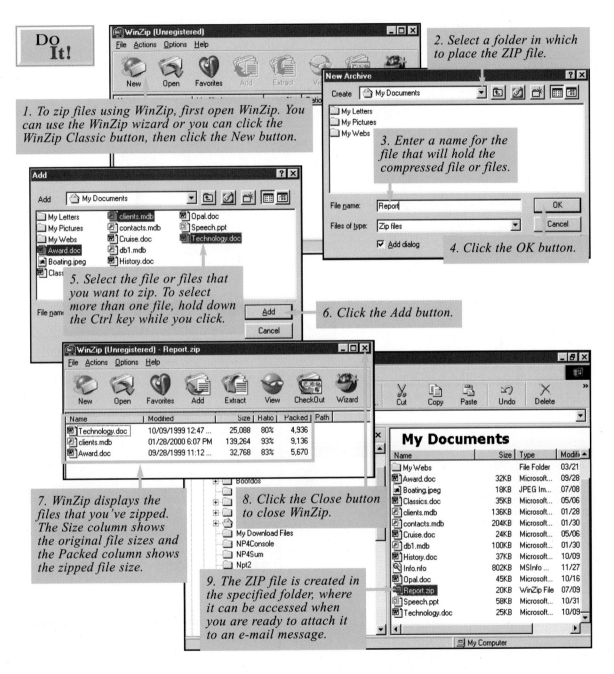

Do It!

1. To zip files using WinZip, first open WinZip. You can use the WinZip wizard or you can click the WinZip Classic button, then click the New button.

2. Select a folder in which to place the ZIP file.

3. Enter a name for the file that will hold the compressed file or files.

4. Click the OK button.

5. Select the file or files that you want to zip. To select more than one file, hold down the Ctrl key while you click.

6. Click the Add button.

7. WinZip displays the files that you've zipped. The Size column shows the original file sizes and the Packed column shows the zipped file size.

8. Click the Close button to close WinZip.

9. The ZIP file is created in the specified folder, where it can be accessed when you are ready to attach it to an e-mail message.

■ Files in some formats are already compressed and typically won't shrink further when zipped. Files formats that don't compress well include .jpg, .jpeg, and .gif graphics and most video formats such as .avi and .mpeg files.

■ Some file formats shrink significantly when zipped, including word processing document .doc files, database .mdb files, and .bmp graphics files.

■FAQ How do I unzip files?

ZIP files typically have a .zip file name extension. Before you can view the contents of these files, you'll need to unzip them. When you unzip a file, WinZip restores the file or files to their original size and stores them under their original names. When this process is complete and the files are back in their original formats, you can delete the ZIP file.

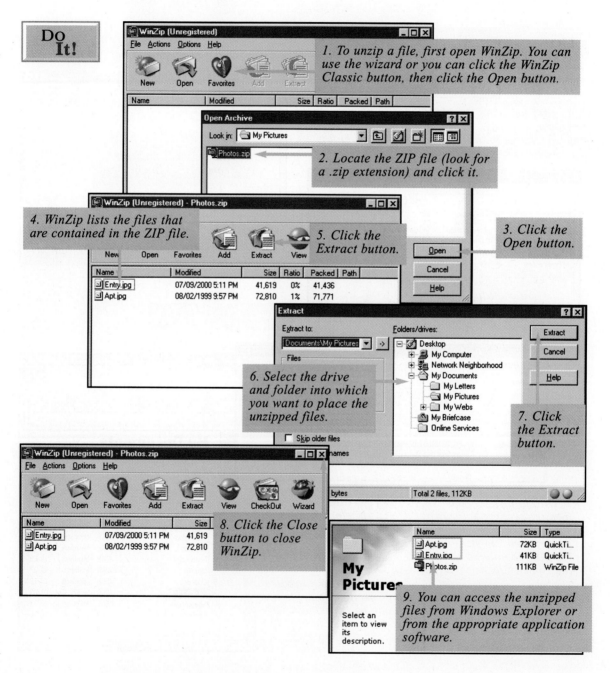

1. To unzip a file, first open WinZip. You can use the wizard or you can click the WinZip Classic button, then click the Open button.

2. Locate the ZIP file (look for a .zip extension) and click it.

3. Click the Open button.

4. WinZip lists the files that are contained in the ZIP file.

5. Click the Extract button.

6. Select the drive and folder into which you want to place the unzipped files.

7. Click the Extract button.

8. Click the Close button to close WinZip.

9. You can access the unzipped files from Windows Explorer or from the appropriate application software.

■ Some users find it helpful to place all ZIP files in a special folder, so that they always know where to find them.

■ When you unzip a file, you'll often want to place the unzipped files in a different folder than the original ZIP file. To do so, make sure that you select the new destination folder in step 6 above.

■ ■ ■

■FAQ How can I get an FTP program for my computer?

FTP (file transfer protocol) is a standard technology that's used to transfer files from one computer to another over the Internet. You can use an FTP program to locate files on a server, download files from a server, or upload files from your computer to a server. FTP is the preferred way to send or receive very large files—those over 5 megabytes in size.

WS_FTP is one of the most popular FTP programs. You can use your browser to download a free, individual-use version of this software called WS_FTP LE.

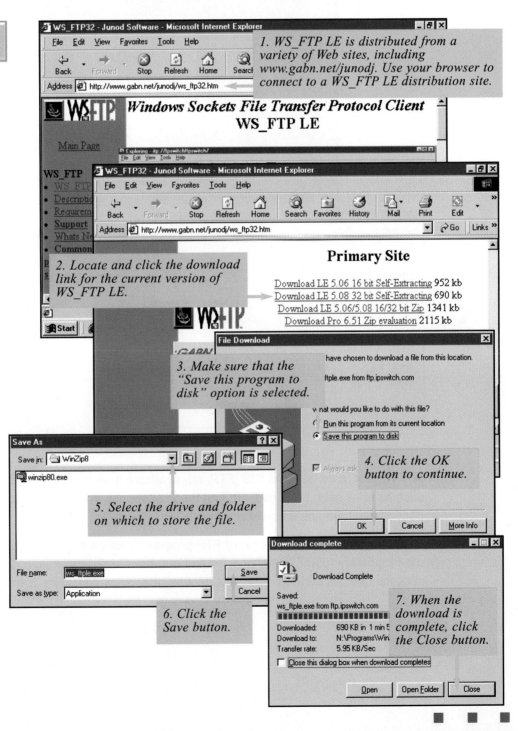

1. WS_FTP LE is distributed from a variety of Web sites, including www.gabn.net/junodj. Use your browser to connect to a WS_FTP LE distribution site.

2. Locate and click the download link for the current version of WS_FTP LE.

3. Make sure that the "Save this program to disk" option is selected.

4. Click the OK button to continue.

5. Select the drive and folder on which to store the file.

6. Click the Save button.

7. When the download is complete, click the Close button.

■ How can I get an FTP program for my computer? (continued)

After WS_FTP LE has been downloaded to your computer, you'll need to complete the automated installation routine.

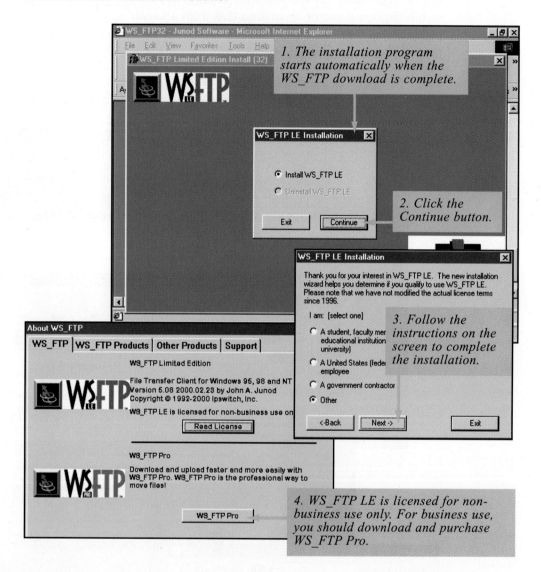

■ FTP programs, such as WS_FTP, are available from a number of Web sites such as www.gabn.net/junodj. To find these sites, use your browser and a Web-based search engine to look for either "FTP software" or "WS_FTP."

■ AOL users can use a standard FTP program such as WS_FTP, or they can use the proprietary AOL FTP service. To find out more about the AOL FTP service, click the Internet button on the AOL toolbar, then click FTP (File Transfer).

■FAQ How do I download files using FTP?

You'll probably use FTP more often to download files than to upload them, so let's look at the downloading procedure first. When you **download** a file, you are transferring a copy of it from one computer—usually a server—to your own computer.

To download a file using FTP, you need to know the address of the FTP server on which the file is stored. Typically, these server addresses begin with "ftp," as in ftp.microsoft.com or ftp.aol.com. Some FTP sites allow anyone to connect and download files, usually as what's called an "anonymous user." Other FTP sites can be accessed only if you have a valid user ID and password.

Do It!

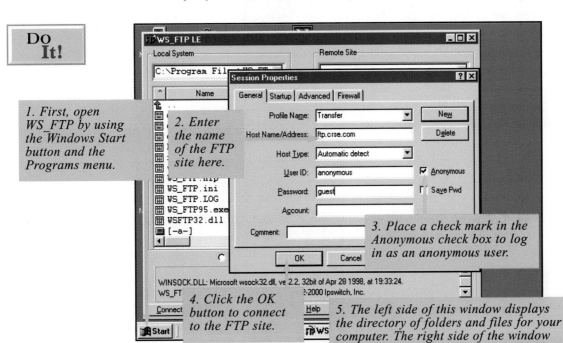

1. First, open WS_FTP by using the Windows Start button and the Programs menu.

2. Enter the name of the FTP site here.

3. Place a check mark in the Anonymous check box to log in as an anonymous user.

4. Click the OK button to connect to the FTP site.

5. The left side of this window displays the directory of folders and files for your computer. The right side of the window displays the directory for the FTP server.

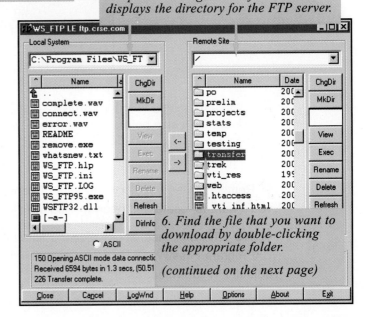

6. Find the file that you want to download by double-clicking the appropriate folder.

(continued on the next page)

■ How do I download files using FTP? (continued)

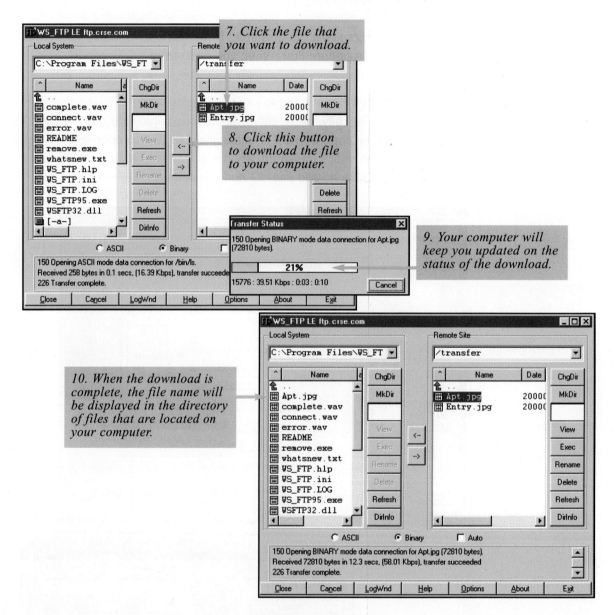

■ It can take a long time to download a large file over a slow dial-up connection. Check the file's size before you start to download a file. Files over 1 megabyte in size will take several minutes to download. Files over 10 megabytes can take many hours to download.

■ Remember the directory and folder into which you download the file because you'll want to locate and open the file after you've downloaded it.

■ WS_FTP will place all downloaded files into a default folder, typically C:\Program Files\WS_FTP. If you can't find your file after downloading, check the default FTP download folder.

■ If a download is interrupted for any reason, it might be possible to restart the download. Reconnect to the Internet if needed, start WS_FTP, then reconnect to the FTP site from which you were downloading the file.

▪FAQ How do I send files using FTP?

When you **upload** a file, you transfer it from your computer to an FTP server on the Internet. Most FTP servers will not let just anyone upload files—you'll typically need a user ID and password in order to upload a file. Check with your ISP to see if it provides an FTP server and folders where you can upload files.

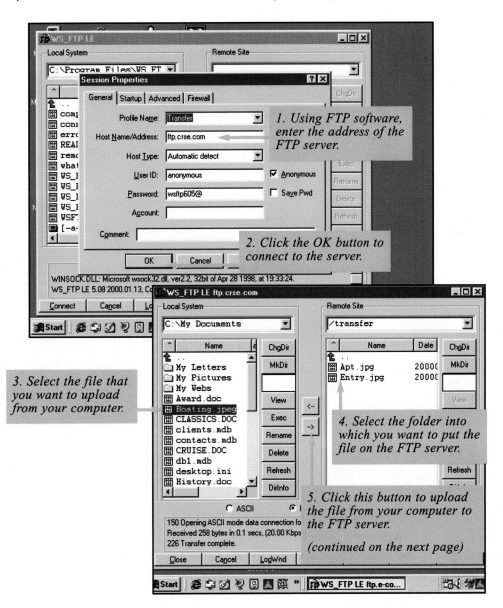

1. Using FTP software, enter the address of the FTP server.

2. Click the OK button to connect to the server.

3. Select the file that you want to upload from your computer.

4. Select the folder into which you want to put the file on the FTP server.

5. Click this button to upload the file from your computer to the FTP server.

(continued on the next page)

■ How do I send files using FTP? (continued)

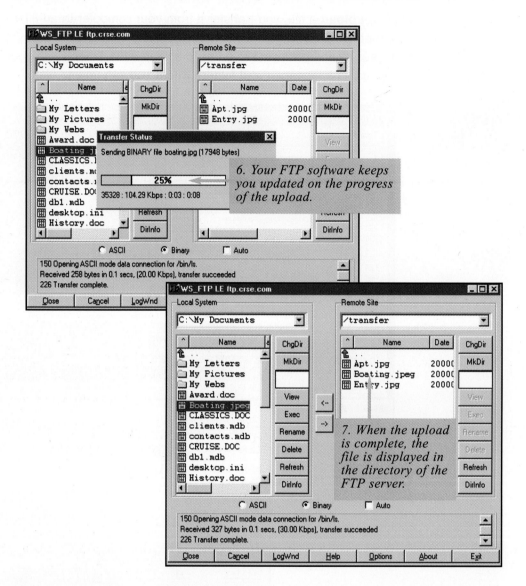

6. *Your FTP software keeps you updated on the progress of the upload.*

7. *When the upload is complete, the file is displayed in the directory of the FTP server.*

■ In most cases, you'll use an FTP server as a halfway point in the process of transferring a file to another person. After you upload a file this other person will be able to download it from the FTP server. You should send an e-mail containing the name and location of the file to the person who is supposed to download it.

■ Space is usually limited on FTP servers. After the file has been successfully uploaded and downloaded, either you or the file recipient should delete the file from the FTP server. To do so, use your FTP program to locate the file on the server, then click the Delete button located on the far right side of the WS_FTP window.

■FAQ How do I use FTP with AOL?

AOL provides its subscribers with a special FTP program. This program is designed to be easier to use than traditional FTP programs, but some users find it more limited and clumsier to use than programs such as WS_FTP.

AOL

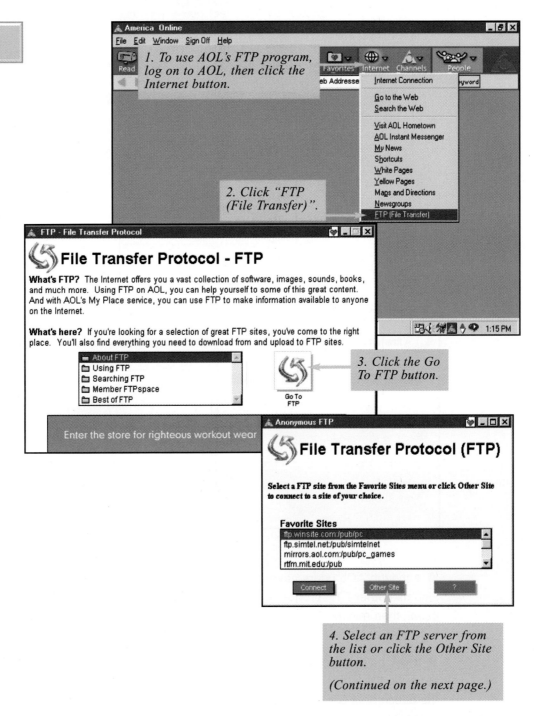

1. To use AOL's FTP program, log on to AOL, then click the Internet button.

2. Click "FTP (File Transfer)".

File Transfer Protocol - FTP

What's FTP? The Internet offers you a vast collection of software, images, sounds, books, and much more. Using FTP on AOL, you can help yourself to some of this great content. And with AOL's My Place service, you can use FTP to make information available to anyone on the Internet.

What's here? If you're looking for a selection of great FTP sites, you've come to the right place. You'll also find everything you need to download from and upload to FTP sites.

3. Click the Go To FTP button.

File Transfer Protocol (FTP)

Select a FTP site from the Favorite Sites menu or click Other Site to connect to a site of your choice.

Favorite Sites

ftp.winsite.com:/pub/pc
ftp.simtel.net:/pub/simtelnet
mirrors.aol.com:/pub/pc_games
rtfm.mit.edu:/pub

4. Select an FTP server from the list or click the Other Site button.

(Continued on the next page.)

■ How do I use FTP with AOL? (continued)

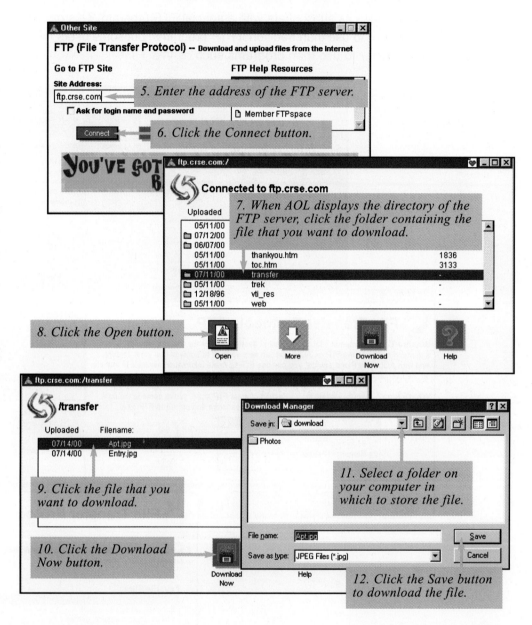

■ Although AOL users have access to the special AOL FTP program, they can also use other FTP programs such as WS_FTP. To do so, connect to AOL as usual, then minimize the AOL window. Start WS_FTP and connect to the FTP server as explained in the previous sections.

■ If you do not specify a folder to hold your downloaded file in step 11, AOL will store the file in the default download directory. For most AOL users, the name of the directory is C:\america online 5.0\download. If you can't find a downloaded file, look for this directory, or one with a similar name, using your computer's Windows Explorer.

∎FAQ How do I join a chat group?

A **chat group** consists of several people who connect to the Internet and communicate by typing comments to each other on their computer keyboards. Chat groups typically take place in "chat rooms" provided by various Web sites, such as AOL and Yahoo!. Some chat groups require you to register before you chat. AOL members can simply "walk into" any AOL chat room, however, and start talking.

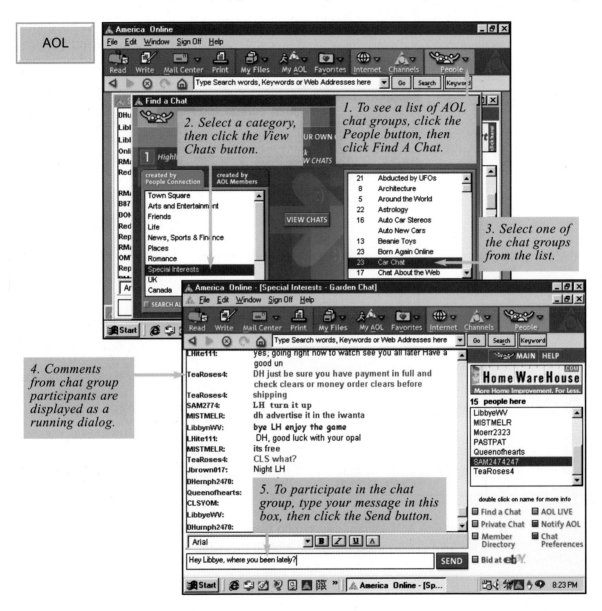

■ Most chat room participants use an alias, or nickname, specifically reserved for chatting. Be careful—many chat room participants are not who they appear to be. Some pose as members of the opposite sex while others pretend to be older or younger than in "real life."

■ Be careful about revealing personal information in a chat group. You never know who the other people in the chat room really are, where they live, or what their intentions might be.

■ ■ ■

■FAQ How does instant messaging work?

Instant messaging is a bit different from chat. With chat, you communicate in real time with anonymous strangers. With **instant messaging**, you communicate privately and in "real time" with one or more of your friends or acquaintances.

Several ISPs, such as AOL and MSN provide instant messaging tools. How do you know when your friends are online? You can add your friends to your instant messaging list and you'll be notified automatically when they come online.

AOL

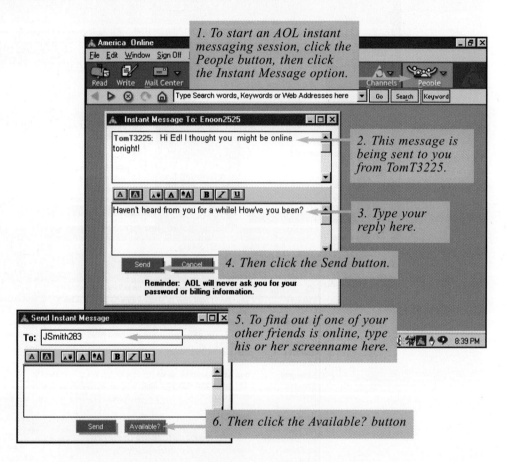

1. To start an AOL instant messaging session, click the People button, then click the Instant Message option.

2. This message is being sent to you from TomT3225.

3. Type your reply here.

4. Then click the Send button.

5. To find out if one of your other friends is online, type his or her screenname here.

6. Then click the Available? button

■ You can use AOL instant messaging even if you aren't an AOL member. Check www.aol.com to download the latest instant messaging software.

■ Although AOL was one of the first services to popularize instant messaging, it isn't the only instant messaging service available. Microsoft offers a competing instant messaging service. Find out more about Microsoft instant messaging at http://messenger.msn.com or www.msn.com.

■ Can you send instant messages between AOL's service and Microsoft's service? The answer, unfortunately, is "sometimes." New versions of AOL's instant messaging software don't always communicate with Microsoft's software. The best advice is to try it, but don't depend on it to work.

QuickCheck A

1. When you use FTP to _____ a file, you send it from your computer to an FTP server on the Internet.

2. True or false? If you want to send a file to a friend using FTP, you would typically upload it directly to his or her hard disk drive. _____

3. True or false? You can use a program such as WinZip to compress one or more files into a single compressed file that is typically smaller than the original files. _____

4. A(n) _____ group allows you to communicate in real-time with a number of anonymous users over the Internet.

5. Instant _____ allows you to communicate privately with one or more of your online friends.

Check It!

QuickCheck B

Indicate the letter of the screen element that best matches the following:

1. The button that you use to create a ZIP file ____

2. The button that unzips the files listed ____

3. The original name of a file contained in the ZIP file ____

4. The original size of a file contained in the ZIP file ____

5. The button that displays the contents of a ZIP file ____

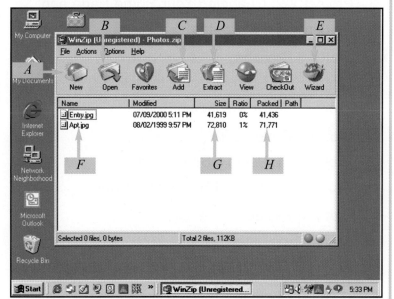

Check It!

Get It?

Skill Set A: Using FTP   Skill Set C: Using Chat

Skill Set B: Using WinZip

Projects

■ ■ ■

■Introduction to Projects

The projects in this section are designed to help you review and develop the skills that you learned in each chapter of this book. They serve as a valuable intermediate step between the *The Practical Internet* learning environment and working on your own. Even if they have not been assigned by your instructor, you'll find that trying some of the projects will greatly enhance your ability to use an Internet browser and e-mail software.

Although it was not required for interacting with the screen tours in Chapters 1–7 to complete the projects, you will need to have Internet access, a browser, e-mail software, and an active e-mail account. You'll find additional information on locating, downloading, and configuring your software on the next few pages.

If you don't remember how to complete a task for a project, refer to *The Practical Internet* book. It is designed to serve as a convenient reference guide to the skills that you've learned—keep it handy as you work on the projects and when working on your own.

Most projects require you to create a file and save it on disk. You can save these projects files on the hard disk of your personal computer or on a floppy disk.

At the completion of each project, you'll have created a file that demonstrates your ability to apply your Internet browser and e-mail application skills. To submit a completed project to your instructor, use one of the methods indicated by the instructions at the end of the project. Most projects can be printed, saved to a disk, or sent as an e-mail attachment. Your instructor might have a preference for one of these methods. You'll find additional information about printing, saving, and e-mailing projects on the next pages.

■Getting an Internet Connection

You'll need an Internet connection to complete the projects. If you already subscribe to an ISP, or if your school or business has provided you with an Internet connection, you're all set. If your computer does not yet have an Internet connection, you should refer to Chapter 1 for information on selecting an ISP, installing and connecting a modem (if necessary), and connecting to the Internet.

■Configuring Your Browser Software

You can complete the projects using any of the popular browsers covered in this book—AOL, Internet Explorer, or Netscape Navigator. To discover if you have a browser already installed on your computer, look for one of the browser icons (AOL), (Internet Explorer), or (Netscape Navigator) on the Windows taskbar at the bottom of your computer screen. You can also check the Programs menu by clicking the Start button, located in the lower left corner of your screen. For additional information on locating your browser, refer to the Chapter 2 FAQ "How do I start my browser?"

If you have no browser installed on your computer, or if you want to make sure that you are using the version that corresponds to the figures in this book, you can download Internet Explorer from www.microsoft.com or Netscape Navigator from www.netscape.com. Note that these files are very large and can take quite a long time to download. The AOL browser is automatically installed when you install the AOL software, which you receive when you subscribe to this ISP.

Many versions of the Internet Explorer, Netscape Navigator, and AOL software exist. The figures in this book were produced using Internet AOL version 5.0, Internet Explorer version 5.0, and Netscape Navigator version 4.7. You can, however, use any version to complete the projects.

Because it is easy to customize the browser window, you might find that your browser looks different than the figures. If you use a computer in a school lab, for example, you might discover that other students change the browser configuration to suit their personal style. The figures were produced on a computer that was set for 640 by 480 screen resolution. If your computer is set for a higher resolution, you might see more buttons and tools across the width of the screen. It is not necessary to change your screen resolution before you work on the projects.

Although it is not necessary for your browser window to look *exactly* like the figures in the book, you might want to display the same toolbars. On the next page, you'll find some tips about configuring the Internet Explorer and Netscape Navigator browser windows.

■ Configuring Your Browser Software (continued)

If you'd like your browser window to look like the figures in this book, check the settings indicated.

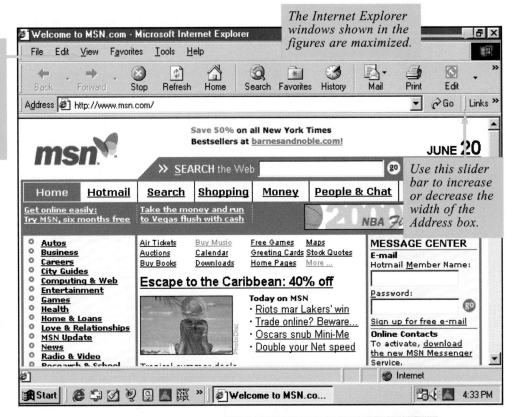

Use the View menu to display or hide the toolbar, Address box, and taskbar.

The Internet Explorer windows shown in the figures are maximized.

Use this slider bar to increase or decrease the width of the Address box.

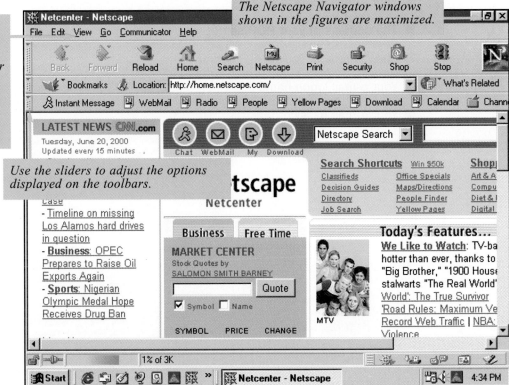

Use the View menu to display or hide the toolbars, Location box, and taskbar.

The Netscape Navigator windows shown in the figures are maximized.

Use the sliders to adjust the options displayed on the toolbars.

■Getting an E-mail Account

You'll need an e-mail account to complete the projects. If you already have an e-mail account provided by your ISP, your school, or your business, you're all set. If you do not yet have an e-mail account, you should obtain one from your ISP or from an Internet mail service, such as Hotmail. Review the first FAQ in Chapter 5 for information about getting an e-mail account.

■Setting Up Your E-mail Software

To maximize your learning experience, you should use one of the e-mail programs discussed in this textbook: AOL Mail, Hotmail, Outlook, or Outlook Express. If your e-mail software was supplied by an ISP, such as AOL, it is probably set up and ready to go. If you have subscribed to Hotmail, you should be set to send and receive mail. If, however, you are using the version of Outlook Express that was shipped with Windows, or the version of Outlook that was included with Microsoft Office, you might have to take additional steps to set up your account.

■Setting Up Outlook or Outlook Express

Before you can use either Outlook or Outlook Express, you'll need to enter your e-mail account information. You can obtain the information from your e-mail provider. You will need to know:

- Your e-mail address
- The address of your POP server
- The address of your SMTP server
- Your e-mail logon name
- Your e-mail password

■ Setting Up Outlook or Outlook Express (continued)

To set up your Outlook or Outlook Express software, you'll need to start it first.
You can then use the Internet Connection Wizard to add your account information.

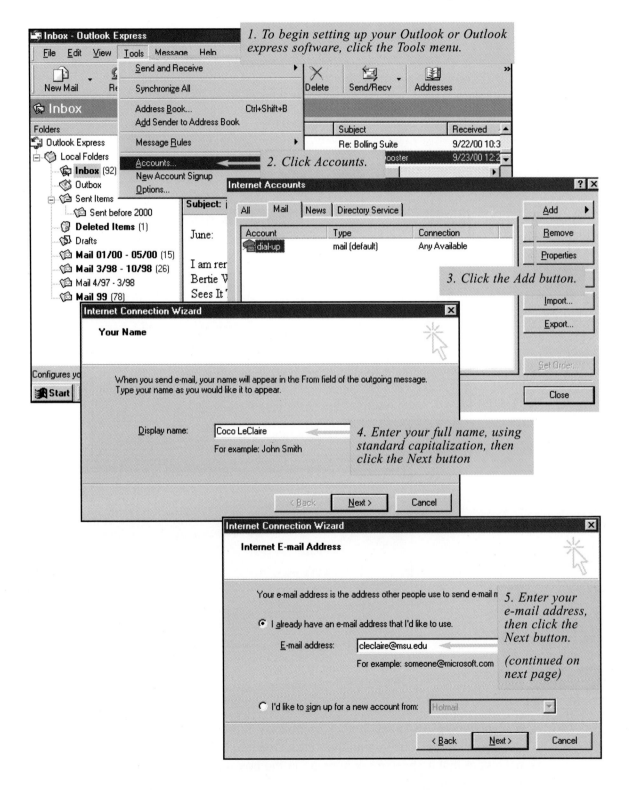

1. To begin setting up your Outlook or Outlook express software, click the Tools menu.

2. Click Accounts.

3. Click the Add button.

4. Enter your full name, using standard capitalization, then click the Next button

5. Enter your e-mail address, then click the Next button.

(continued on next page)

■ Setting Up Outlook or Outlook Express (continued)

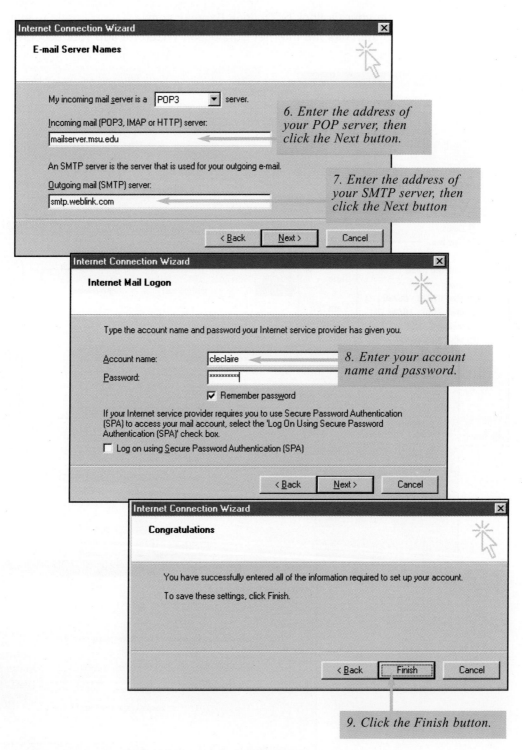

6. *Enter the address of your POP server, then click the Next button.*

7. *Enter the address of your SMTP server, then click the Next button*

8. *Enter your account name and password.*

9. *Click the Finish button.*

■ If you would like to set Outlook or Outlook Express to automatically check your spelling, click the Tools menu, then click Options. Select the Spelling tab and make sure that a check mark appears in the box *Always check spelling before sending.* You might also want a check mark in the box *Suggest replacements for misspelled words.*

■Submitting an Assignment as a Printout, on Disk, or as an E-mail Attachment

■ To print a project file:

1. Make sure that a printer is attached to your computer and that it is turned on.

2. Click the Print button or click File, then click Print.

3. If the printout doesn't already include your name, student ID, section number, and date, be sure to write this information on the printout.

■ To save your file on a floppy disk:

1. Click the Save As option on the File menu.

2. When the Save As dialog box appears, use the ▼ button on the *Save in* box to select 3½ Floppy (A:).

3. In the *File name* box, enter the name specified by the project instructions.

4. Click the Save button to complete the process.

5. Before you submit your disk to your instructor, make sure that you've labeled it with the project name, your name, your student ID, your section number, and date.

■ To send your project as an e-mail attachment:

First make sure that you have saved the project file. Next, start your e-mail software. Then, follow your software's procedures for sending an e-mail attachment. The procedure usually consists of the following steps:

1. Start a new message by using a toolbar button, such as Compose Message (Outlook Express) or Write Mail (AOL Mail).

2. Address the new message to your instructor.

3. Enter your student ID number, the project number, and your class section in the subject line.

4. Click the Attachment button or select the Attachment option from a menu.

5. When prompted, specify the disk that contains the attachment—usually 3½ Floppy (A:)—and then select the project file from the list.

6. Click the Send button to send the e-mail message and attachment.

■Project 1-1: Gathering Computer System Information

Various ISPs offer different connection speeds and support options. They also might accommodate different operating systems and run a different selection of browser and e-mail software packages.

To select the ISP that is best for you, it is useful to know your computer's specifications. For example, if you know your computer's operating system, you will know whether to request your ISP's software for Windows 3.x, Windows 95/98, Windows 2000, or the Mac operating system. Knowing your computer's processor speed will help you to decide if the software you request will run at a sufficient speed on your system. Likewise, determining your computer's hard disk capacity will help you to decide if your computer has enough disk space to install and run the ISP software. Finally, if you know your modem speed, you will be able to decide if the ISP can offer you a connection that optimizes your modem capabilities.

In this project you will gather specifications about your computer system that are important to know before selecting an ISP.

Requirements for this project: This assignment requires Microsoft Windows. Microsoft Word 2000 is optional.

Project files needed: No supplemental student files are needed.

To discover your computer's operating system version, processor speed, and RAM capacity, complete Steps 1 through 4:

1. Start your computer and click the Start button. Select the Settings menu and then select Control Panel.

2. In the Control Panel window, double-click the System icon.

3. In the System Properties window, make sure that you have selected the General tab.

4. Write down your computer's operating system, processor speed, and RAM capacity, then close this window.

■ ■ ■

■ Project 1-1 (continued)

To find out the amount of disk space that's available on your computer, complete Steps 5 through 6.

5. Double-click the My Computer icon. Right-click the C: (hard disk drive) icon. Select the Properties option, and then make sure that you have selected the General tab.

6. Write down your computer's free space. (It is the pink area.)

To find out your computer's modem speed, complete Steps 7 through 9.

7. Click the Start button, point to Settings, then select Control Panel.

8. In the Control Panel window, double-click the Modems icon. Make sure that you have selected the General tab.

9. Write down your computer's modem speed.

10. Use one of the following methods to submit your answers from Steps 4, 6, and 9 on paper, on disk, or as an email attachment:

■ To submit your assignment manually, on paper, simply write your answers on paper and label them 4, 6, and 9. Make sure that you include your name, section number, date, and "Project 1-1." To submit your assignment as a paper printout, first open a word processing program, such as Microsoft Word or WordPad. Type your name and "Project 1-1." Type your answers and label them 4, 6, and 9. Save the file as Project 1-1 XXXX 9999, where XXXX is your student ID number and 9999 is your class section number. Use the Print option from the File menu to print your document.

■ To submit your assignment on disk, open a word processing program, such as Microsoft Word or WordPad. Type your name and "Project 1-1." Type your answers and label them 4, 6, and 9. Save the file as Project 1-1 XXXX 9999, where XXXX is your student ID number and 9999 is your class section number.

■ To submit your assignment as an e-mail message, open your e-mail software and start a new message. Type your instructor's address in the To: box. Click the Subject box, then type Project 1-1, your student ID number, and your class section number. For the body of the message, type your answers to Steps 4, 6, and 9. Click the Send button or perform any additional steps required by your e-mail software to send an e-mail message.

■Project 1-2: Selecting an Internet Service Provider

In Project 1-1, you determined your computer's specifications, such as its operating system, processor speed, RAM capacity, hard disk capacity, and modem speed. In this project, you will develop the knowledge necessary to research various ISPs. This activity will help you to determine which ISP is best for your computing and Internet needs.

Requirements for this project: This assignment requires Microsoft Windows. Microsoft Word 2000 is optional.

Project files needed: No supplemental student files are needed.

1. Your first task is to make a list of ISPs that service your area. You can use any of the following strategies to create a list of potential ISPs:

- Ask your friends and relatives which ISP they use.
- Look in the yellow pages of your local phone book under "Internet" or "Computers."
- Scan newspapers, magazines, television, and other media resources for local or national ISPs.
- If you are already online, browse the Internet for ISPs. Some sites may offer free downloads or trial offers.

2. Now that you have a list of possible ISPs, contact two of them and ask about features, billing rates, and system requirements. Most ISPs offer e-mail, newsgroup access, chat, instant messaging, and Web hosting. The following list includes some questions that you might want to ask an ISP:

- Are customers required to pay a setup or installation fee?
- What system requirements are needed to effectively run the ISP software?
- What is the customer-to-modem ratio? Meaning, how does the number of ISP customers compare to the number of modems provided by the ISP? The higher the ratio, the less likely the ISP will slow down with heavy Internet traffic.
- Are technical support services available to customers? If so, are they available by phone and/or Web site? What are the hours and response times? Note: If your Internet connection is not working, you will not be able to use e-mail or a Web site to get technical support. Also, if you have trouble with your Internet connection when your ISP's technical support department is closed, you will have to wait for assistance.
- Can customers purchase the service month-to-month, annually, or at an hourly rate? What is the cost for each?

■ Project 1-2 (continued)

3. Once you have researched at least two ISPs, write a brief summary of which ISP you would select and why. In making your selection, you might want to consider what you learned in the Chapter 1 FAQ "How do I select an ISP?" such as:

■ Flat rates are usually the best option if you plan to spend a lot of time on the Internet.

■ Be very careful of "free" ISP offers. They usually have some sort of "angle," like unwanted advertising that appears on your screen, which requires longer downloading time.

■ National ISPs are a good choice if you travel frequently. They often provide toll-free and local access numbers that will help you to avoid paying long distance connection rates.

4. Use one of the following methods to submit your summary on paper, on disk, or as an email attachment, according to your instructor's directions:

■ To submit your assignment manually, on paper, simply write your summary on paper and label it "ISP Summary." Make sure that you include your name, section number, date, and "Project 1-2." To submit your assignment as a paper printout, open a word processing program, such as Microsoft Word or WordPad. Type your name and "Project 1-2." Type your summary. Save the file as Project 1-2 XXXX 9999, where XXXX is your student ID number and 9999 is your class section number. Use the Print option from the File menu to print your document.

■ To submit your assignment on disk, open a word processing program, such as Microsoft Word or WordPad. Type your name and "Project 1-2." Type your summary. Save the file as Project 1-2 XXXX 9999, where XXXX is your student ID number and 9999 is your class section number.

■ To submit your assignment as an e-mail attachment, open a word processing program, such as Microsoft Word or WordPad. Type your name and "Project 1-2." Type your summary. Save the file as Project 1-2 XXXX 9999, where XXXX is your student ID number and 9999 is your class section number. Open your e-mail software. Type your instructor's address in the To: box. Click the Subject box, then type Project 1-2, your student ID number, and your class section number. Attach the Project 1-2 file. Click the Send button or perform any additional steps required by your e-mail software to send an e-mail message.

■Project 2-1: Using a Browser

This project will help you to apply the basic navigation skills needed to successfully surf the Internet.

Requirements for this project: This assignment requires Microsoft Windows and either Internet Explorer or Netscape Navigator.

Project files needed: No supplemental student files are needed.

1. Start your browser and connect to the site http://www.e-course.com/mgh/ What does the title bar show as the title of this site?

2. Once at the site, click the Mardi Gras link. Add this page to your Favorites or Bookmarks. How many sites are listed in your Favorites/Bookmarks list?

3. Use the Back button to return to the original Mardi Gras Hotel page, then select the Accommodations link. Which of the Hotel's suites would you reserve if you were going to stay in the hotel?

4. Use the Back button to return to the main hotel page, then select the Reservations link. What does the title bar show as the title of this page?

5. Use the Back button to return to the main hotel page. How many times did you have to click the Back button?

6. Use the Forward button to return to the Reservations page, then scroll down to the bottom of this page. Is the online reservation system up and running?

■ Project 2-1 (continued)

7. Connect to the site www.ross-simons.com. Click the Stop button. Did the entire page load?

8. Can you access the site www.mardigras.com from your history list? Explain why or why not.

9. Use one of the following methods to submit your responses to the questions in Steps 1 through 8 on paper, on disk, or as an e-mail attachment, according to your instructor's directions:

■ To submit your assignment manually, on paper, simply write your answers on paper and label each answer with the corresponding number. Make sure that you include your name, section number, date, and "Project 2-1."

■ To submit your assignment as a paper printout, open a word processing program, such as Microsoft Word or WordPad. Type your name and "Project 2-1." Type your answers, labeled 1 through 9. Save the file as Project 2-1 XXXX 9999, where XXXX is your student ID number and 9999 is your class section number. Use the Print option from the File menu to print your document.

■ To submit your assignment on disk, open a word processing program, such as Microsoft Word or WordPad. Type your name and "Project 2-1." Type your answers, labeled 1 through 9. Save the file as Project 2-1 XXXX 9999, where XXXX is your student ID number and 9999 is your class section number.

■ To submit your assignment as an e-mail attachment, open a word processing program, such as Microsoft Word or WordPad. Type your name and "Project 2-1." Type your answers, labeled 1 through 9. Save the file as Project 2-1 XXXX 9999, where XXXX is your student ID number and 9999 is your class section number. Type your instructor's address in the To: box. Click the Subject box, then type Project 2-1, your student ID number, and your class section number. Attach your Project 2-1 file to the e-mail message. Click the Send button or perform any additional steps required by your e-mail software to send an e-mail message.

▪Project 2-2: Changing Your Home Page and Working with Favorites

In this project, you will change your home page. Additionally, you will gain experience adding and removing interesting Web sites to and from your Favorites menu.

Requirements for this project: This assignment requires Microsoft Windows, Microsoft Word, and either Internet Explorer or Netscape Navigator.

Project files needed: No supplemental student files are needed.

1. Start your browser. When your browser opens, the page displayed is your home page.

2. Change your home page to www.msnbc.com. What is the full name of this site? What are some of the advantages and disadvantages of having this site as your home page.

3. Browse through some of the links on the MSNBC site.

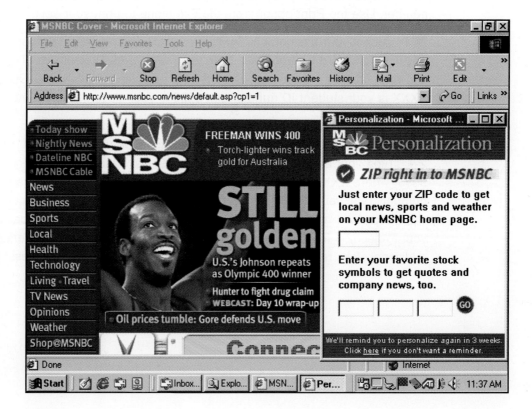

4. Find two Web page links that interest you and add them to your Favorites list. What are the URLs for these sites?

5. Use the Home button to return to your MSNBC home page.

6. Use the Favorites list to return to the first page that you added to the Favorites list in Step 4.

■ Project 2-2 (continued)

7. Open the Favorites list again and remove the second page that you added in Step 4.

8. In your own words, describe the steps for adding and removing a site to the Favorites list.

9. Use one of the following methods to submit your responses for Steps 2, 3, and 8 on paper, on disk, or as an email attachment, according to your instructor's directions:

■ To submit your assignment manually on paper, simply write your answers on paper and label them 2, 3, and 10. Make sure that you include your name, section number, date, and "Project 2-2."

■ To submit your assignment as a paper printout, open a word processing program, such as Microsoft Word or WordPad. Type your name and "Project 2-2." Type your answers and label them 2, 3, and 10. Save the file as Project 2-2 XXXX 9999, where XXXX is your student ID number and 9999 is your class section number. Use the Print option from the File menu to print your document.

■ To submit your assignment on disk, open a word processing program, such as Microsoft Word or WordPad. Type your name and "Project 2-2." Type your answers and label them 2, 3, and 10. Save the file as Project 2-2 XXXX 9999, where XXXX is your student ID number and 9999 is your class section number.

■ To submit your assignment as an e-mail attachment, open a word processing program, such as Microsoft Word or WordPad. Type your name and "Project 2-2." Type your answers and label them 2, 3, and 10. Save the file as Project 2-2 XXXX 9999, where XXXX is your student ID number and 9999 is your class section number. Open your e-mail software and start a new message. Type your instructor's address in the To: box. Click the Subject box, then type Project 2-2, your student ID number, and your class section number. Attach the Project 2-2 document. Click the Send button or perform any additional steps required by your e-mail software to send an e-mail message.

■Project 3-1: Buying Products Online

In this project you will gain hands-on practice purchasing merchandise online.

Requirements for this project: This assignment requires Microsoft Windows and either Internet Explorer or Netscape Navigator.

Project files needed: No supplemental student files are needed.

1. Start your browser and explore the Web sites for online computer vendors, such as www.pcconnection.com, www.dell.com, or www.microwarehouse.com. After browsing for awhile, choose one site and compare prices for three color ink-jet printers.

2. Write down the brand and model number for the two least expensive printers.

3. Add one of these printers to your shopping cart.

4. Now, suppose that you also need a cable to connect the printer to your computer. Does the site help you find the correct cable? If possible, add a printer cable to your shopping cart. (If the site does not make any suggestions, look for a parallel printer cable.)

5. Continue as if you are going to purchase the printer and the cable, until you see a page that displays the total cost of your order, including shipping. Make a note of the printer price, the cable price, the tax, the shipping cost, and the total price.

6. Delete both items from your shopping cart, then leave the site.

7. Summarize your activities for this project by answering the following questions:

a. What was the name of the Web site that you used to compare printers?

b. What were the brands and model numbers for the two least expensive printers?

c. Which printer did you add to your shopping cart?

d. What were the prices for the printer, cable, tax, shipping, and order total?

8. Use one of the following methods to submit your project results from Steps 3 and 6 on paper, on disk, or as an email attachment, according to your instructor's directions:

■ To submit your assignment manually, simply write your answers to questions 1 through 4 on paper. Make sure that you include your name, section number, date, and "Project 3-1."

■ Project 3-1 (continued)

■ To submit your assignment as a paper printout, open a word processing program, such as Microsoft Word or WordPad. Type your name and "Project 3-1." Type your answers to questions 1 through 4. Save the file as Project 3-1 XXXX 9999, where XXXX is your student ID number and 9999 is your class section number. Use the Print option from the File menu to print your document.

■ To submit your assignment on disk, open a word processing program, such as Microsoft Word or WordPad. Type your name and "Project 3-1." Type your answers for questions 1 through 4. Save the file as Project 3-1 XXXX 9999, where XXXX is your student ID number and 9999 is your class section number.

■ To submit your assignment as an e-mail attachment, open a word processing program, such as Microsoft Word or WordPad. Type your name and "Project 3-1." Type your answers for questions 1 through 4. Save the file as Project 3-1 XXXX 9999, where XXXX is your student ID number and 9999 is your class section number. Open your e-mail software and start a new message. Type your instructor's address in the To: box. Click the Subject box, then type Project 3-1, your student ID number, and your class section number. Attach the Project 3-1 file. Click the Send button or perform any additional steps required by your e-mail software to send an e-mail message.

■Project 3-2: Downloading Software

In this project you will download and install the RealPlayer—software that you can use to play sound and video files.

Requirements for this project: This assignment requires Microsoft Windows and either Internet Explorer or Netscape Navigator. If you are planning to complete this project on a school or business computer, make sure that you have permission to download and install software on that computer.

Project files needed: No supplemental student files are needed.

1. Use your browser to connect to the Web site www.real.com. What is the name of the company that operates this Web site?

2. The time required for your download depends upon the speed of your Internet connection. To discover your connection speed, click the Dial-Up Connection icon in the lower-right corner of the Windows desktop. (Students with AOL or "always-on" connections should reply to this question by indicating that the connection icon was not available.) What is the speed of your Internet connection?

3. Locate the download link for the most recent version of the RealPlayer software. What is the number of the most recent version?

4. Look for the minimum system requirements for the RealPlayer software and write them down. Is your computer capable of running this software?

5. Complete the online form required before downloading this software. Do you have an opportunity to select or reject additional promotional offers from this company?

6. Download the software and keep track of the time required to do so. How long did it take to download the RealPlayer?

7. Compare your connection speed and download time with those of your classmates. Did the person with the fastest connection also have the fastest download time? Explain your answer.

8. If it is permitted, install the RealPlayer on your computer. Does the installation process create an entry on the Start/Programs menu? Does it create an icon on the Windows desktop?

9. Use one of the following methods to submit your project results from Steps 1 through 8 on paper, on disk, or as an email attachment, according to your instructor's directions:

■ To submit your assignment manually, simply write your answers on paper after the appropriate question number. Make sure that you include your name, section number, date, and "Project 3-2."

■ Project 3-2 (continued)

■ To submit your assignment as a paper printout, open a word processing program, such as Microsoft Word or WordPad. Type your name and "Project 3-2." Type your answers and label each one with the corresponding question number. Save the file as Project 3-2 XXXX 9999, where XXXX is your student ID number and 9999 is your class section number. Use the Print option from the File menu to print your document.

■ To submit your assignment on disk, open a word processing program, such as Microsoft Word or WordPad. Type your name and "Project 3-2." Type your answers and label each one with the question number. Save the file as Project 3-2 XXXX 9999, where XXXX is your student ID number and 9999 is your class section number.

■ To submit your assignment as an e-mail attachment, open a word processing program, such as Microsoft Word or WordPad. Type your name and "Project 3-2." Type your answers and label each one with the question number. Save the file as Project 3-2 XXXX 9999, where XXXX is your student ID number and 9999 is your class section number. Open your e-mail software and start a new message. Type your instructor's address in the To: box. Click the Subject box, then type Project 3-2, your student ID number, and your class section number. Attach the Project 3-2 file. Click the Send button or perform any additional steps required by your e-mail software to send an e-mail message.

■Project 4-1: Using a Search Engine

This project will help you become a savvy Internet information consumer. You will use search engines to locate and evaluate the content of several different Web sites as potential research resources.

Requirements for this project: This assignment requires Microsoft Windows, either Internet Explorer or Netscape Navigator; and either Word 2000 or Excel 2000.

Project files needed: No supplemental student files are needed.

1. Use your browser to connect to one of the many available search engines described in Chapter 4, such as Yahoo!, Google, or Excite.

2. Use a Word processor or electronic spreadsheet to create a table like the one shown in the sample below.

	Web Site 1	Web Site 2	Web Site 3
Site URL			
Date visited			
Site category			
Title			
Date written or posted			
Author			
Credentials			
Purpose			
Reference citations or Links provided to supporting sites?			
Clearly written?			
E-mail contact?			
Opinions clearly separated from facts?			

3. Using the following points as a guide, locate and evaluate three Web sites with regard to their suitability as sources of research information. For each site, fill in one of the columns in the table that you created in Step 2.

■ It is good practice to write down the page's URL, the date that you visited it, and a brief description of why you would or would not return to the site. Doing so will help you later if you decide to use the site as a resource for a research paper.

■ Most sites can be categorized as commercial (operated by a commercial business), academic (written by an instructor or student at a university), news (operated by news bureau, such as ABC, NBC, or Reuters), government (maintained by a government agency), personal (written by an individual), or professional (written by a member of a professional group, such as the

■ Project 4-1 (continued)

Association for Computing Machinery). The quality of the information on a Web page tends to be more reliable when the page is maintained by a professional news organization, a government agency, or a professional group. Although it is a good idea to cross check information with other sources, you should be especially careful to do so when using information from a personal or commercial Web site.

■ It is important to determine the author of a Web site. It could be an individual or an organization. Always look for the author's credentials or qualifications to verify the quality and authenticity of the Web site's information. You may need to be cautious about the ideas expressed on a personal Web site or a commercial Web site.

■ It is extremely important that the author clearly distinguishes opinions from facts.

■ The purpose of a Web page is not always simply to provide information. Some Web page authors want to influence your opinions or affect your buying habits. If you understand the underlying purpose of a Web page, you can view its contents within that context.

■ Determine if the page includes links to sources that verify its information. If the site does not have supportive links use caution and cross check with other resources.

■ The concepts represented should be clear and supported by outside sources or other reputable businesses or persons.

■ Notice the copyright date, date of publication, or last update. You would not want to assume that the information is current when in fact it could be outdated material.

■ Navigation within a site should be user-friendly—a typical user should be able to move from page to page at the site without getting confused or lost.

■ It is a good sign of quality control and authenticity of information if the page offers a link to a contact person.

4. Use one of the following methods to submit your Web site evaluation table on paper, on disk, or as an e-mail attachment:

■ To submit your assignment manually, simply create your table on paper and fill it in. Make sure that you include your name, section number, date, and "Project 4-1."

■ To submit your assignment as a paper printout, open a word processing program, such as Microsoft Word or WordPad. Type your name and "Project 4-1." Create the table and fill it in. Save the file as Project 4-1 XXXX 9999, where XXXX is your student ID number and 9999 is your class section number. Use the Print option from the File menu to print your document.

■ To submit your assignment on disk, create the table and fill it in using a word processing program. Save the file as Project 4-1 XXXX 9999, where XXXX is your student ID number and 9999 is your class section number.

■ To submit your assignment as an e-mail attachment, create the table and fill it in using a word processing program. Type your name and "Project 4-1." Save the file as Project 4-1 XXXX 9999, where XXXX is your student ID number and 9999 is your class section number. Attach the file to an e-mail message addressed to your instructor. In the Subject box enter Project 4-1, your student ID number, and your class section number. Attach the Project 4-1 file and then send the message.

■Project 4-2: Internet Scavenger Hunt

In this project you will explore the Internet "jungle" to find information on various topics.

Requirements for this project: This assignment requires Microsoft Windows, Microsoft Word, and either Internet Explorer or Netscape Navigator.

Project files needed: No supplemental student files are needed.

Use your browser to connect to one of the many available search engines described in Chapter 4, such as Yahoo!, Google, or Excite. Complete each of the following steps. As you find an answer, write it down. In addition, write down the URL of the Web page on which you found the answer and make a note of the date that you visited the page.

1. What state has the highest mountain?

2. What is the all-time high temperature for Memphis, TN?

3. What is the address, phone number, and e-mail address of your state's governor?

4. What is the area code for Allentown, PA?

5. On January 13 1888, thirty-three people gathered and began organizing the National Geographic Society. Where was this first organizational meeting held?

6. Who were the stars of the movie *Desk Set*?

7. Locate and play a video clip of a current movie. What's the name of the movie and what software opened to play the clip?

8. Monuments are a part of our culture; and most people are familiar with the Washington Monument, Mount Rushmore, the Taj Mahal, and the Eiffel Tower. But, in what city is there a monument to the northern lights?

9. Software designers often include a secret message, program, or graphic called an "Easter egg" in their programs. What steps would you take to look at the driving game Easter egg in the Microsoft Excel 2000 software?

10. As World War II heated up in Europe, U.S. scientists were on the trail of some significant advances in weapons research. Enrico Fermi was the first to actually produce nuclear fission in the laboratory and he won the Nobel Prize for Physics in 1938 for his efforts. On the basis of this work and a supportive letter from Albert Einstein, the U.S. government plunged wholesale into research on creating an atomic bomb. On the brink of success, President Truman used the Potsdam conference to reveal to Stalin that the United States had a new and powerful weapon. Why wasn't Stalin surprised by this news?

■ Project 4-2 (continued)

11. Use one of the following methods to submit your scavenger hunt answers on paper, on disk, or as an e-mail attachment, according to your instructor's directions. Remember to include the URL of the page and the date that you visited the page.

■ To submit your assignment manually, simply write your answers on paper. Make sure that you include your name, section number, date, and "Project 4-2."

■ To submit your assignment as a paper printout, open a word processing program, such as Microsoft Word or WordPad. Type your name and "Project 4-2." Type your answers. Save the file as Project 4-2 XXXX 9999, where XXXX is your student ID number and 9999 is your class section number. Use the Print option from the File menu to print your document.

■ To submit your assignment on disk, open a word processing program, such as Microsoft Word or WordPad. Type your name and "Project 4-2." Type your answers. Save the file as Project 4-2 XXXX 9999, where XXXX is your student ID number and 9999 is your class section number.

■ To submit your assignment as an e-mail attachment, open a word processing program, such as Microsoft Word or WordPad. Type your name and "Project 4-2." Type your answers. Save the file as Project 4-2 XXXX 9999, where XXXX is your student ID number and 9999 is your class section number. Open your e-mail software and start a new message. Type your instructor's address in the To: box. Click the Subject box, then type Project 4-2, your student ID number, and your class section number. Attach the Project 4-2 file. Click the Send button or perform any additional steps required by your e-mail software to send an e-mail message.

■Project 5-1: Using E-mail

In this project you will practice sending, receiving, formatting, and replying to e-mail messages.

Requirements for this project: This assignment requires Microsoft Windows and e-mail software such as Microsoft Outlook or Outlook Express. You will need your instructor's e-mail address.

Project files needed: No supplemental student files are needed.

1. Start your e-mail software.

2. Create a new message to Jack_Hill@cciw.com

3. Enter Great Stock Tip in the subject line and in the message area use your own words to write a short message about the stock market.

4. In the message area, type your name as a closing.

5. Send the message.

6. Now check your mail. You should have a message from Jack_Hill@cciw.com. Reply to this message. Send a copy to your instructor.

■Project 5-2: Browser Plus E-mail

In this project you will have an opportunity to see how your browser can be used together with your e-mail to find addresses and send messages. You'll find the e-mail address of a government representative and send him or her an e-mail message.

Requirements for this project: This assignment requires Microsoft Windows; Internet Explorer or Netscape Navigator; and e-mail software such as Microsoft Outlook or Outlook Express. You will need your instructor's e-mail address.

Project files needed: No supplemental student files are needed.

1. Use your browser to connect to a Web page that lists members of the government for your country:

> United States: www.house.gov
>
> Australia: www.aph.gov.au/house/
>
> New Zealand: www.arraydev.com/commerce/embassy/english/
>
> United Kingdom: www.cabinet-office.gov.uk/
>
> Canada: www.canada.gc.ca/

2. Find the e-mail address of your government representative. You might want to explore the other countries' government sites, too.

3. Open your e-mail software.

4. Compose an e-mail message to your representative regarding some issue that is important to you. You will actually send this message, so write intelligent comments, watch your grammar, and check your spelling. You might want to use your browser to explore some political issues before composing your message.

5. Send a copy of your message to yourself and to your instructor.

6. Make sure that you received your copy of the message.

■Project 6-1: Working with Your Address Book

In this project you will locate e-mail addresses using the e-mail white pages. You will also practice creating and adding contacts/groups to your e-mail address book. Finally, you will familiarize yourself with sending messages to a group.

Requirements for this project: This assignment requires Microsoft Windows, Internet Explorer or Netscape Navigator; and e-mail software such as Outlook, AOL or Hotmail. You will also need your instructor's e-mail address and the e-mail for one of your classmates.

Project files needed: No supplemental student files are needed.

1. Use your browser to connect to one of the many available portal sites, such as Yahoo, Lycos, or Excite.

2. Use one of the "people finder" links to search for your own name.

3. Search for a celebrity such as Denzel Washington or Rosie O'Donnell.

4. Start your e-mail software, open your address book, and add the e-mail address for your celebrity. If you find any additional contact information, enter that in the address book as well.

5. Add the e-mail address for your instructor, a classmate, and yourself. Add other contact information, such as an address and a telephone number.

6. Create a group in your address book named Class Contacts. Include your instructor, your classmate, and your own e-mail address in this group.

7. Compose a brief message and send it to the group that you've designated as Class Contacts.

8. Now check your messages. You should have received your copy.

■Project 6-2: Using E-mail Attachments

In this project you will practice creating documents to use as attachments. Additionally, you will send, view, and save e-mail attachments.

Requirements for this project: This assignment requires Microsoft Windows, Internet Explorer or Netscape Navigator; and e-mail software such as Outlook, AOL or Hotmail. You will also need the Class Contacts group that you added to your address book in Project 6-1.

Project files needed: No supplemental student files are needed.

1. Use your browser to connect to one of the many available search engines such as Yahoo!, Google, or Excite.

2. Search for a Web page and a graphic about a movie that you've seen. Select a small movie graphic and save it as "Movie Graphic."

3. Start your e-mail software and open your address book.

4. Compose a message to the Class Contacts group that describes your opinion of the movie.

5. Attach the "Movie Graphic" file to the message.

6. Send the message.

7. Now check your messages. You should have received your copy of the movie message with its attachment.

8. Open the attachment and view it to make sure that it is the same as the original.

9. Save the attachment as "My Graphic Attachment."

■Project 7-1: Visiting a Chat Room

This project will help you to become a savvy chat participant by exploring chat rooms and evaluating their features.

Requirements for this project: This assignment requires Microsoft Windows, and either Internet Explorer or Netscape Navigator.

Project files needed: No supplemental student files are needed.

1. Use your browser to connect to a portal site that features chat rooms, such as Yahoo!, Lycos, MSN, or Excite.

2. Visit one or more chat rooms until you find one that focuses on topics that are of interest to you. (Please keep it G-rated.) You can participate in the discussion or just "lurk" to see what people are talking about.

3. Write a chat room evaluation by answering the following questions:

■ What is the URL of the chat room that you visited?

■ What was the date and time of your visit?

■ What was the discussion topic?

■ Was there a historical archive for past live chats with famous persons or important topics?

■ How many other people were in the room?

■ Was Help available? If so, did you explore this feature? Was it clear?

■ What language was used in this chat room? Were other languages available?

■ Was the discussion relevant to the topic, or did it wander off to other topics?

■ Did the discussion participants seem to be knowledgeable about the subject?

■ What are your thoughts about your chatting experiences? Did you have difficulties with the process or was it clear and easy to follow? Did you watch or did you chat with others? Would you visit this chat room in the future? Why or why not?

4. Did the chat Web site also provide an instant messenger program? If possible, download the necessary software to use it, then evaluate its ease of use.

■ Project 7-1 (continued)

5. Use one of the following methods to submit your chat room evaluation summary on paper or as an e-mail attachment, according to your instructor's directions:

■ To submit your assignment manually, simply write your summary on paper and title it "Chat Room Evaluation." Make sure that you include your name, section number, date, and "Project 7-1."

■ To submit your assignment as a paper printout, open a word processing program, such as Microsoft Word or WordPad. Type your name and "Project 7-1." Type your summary and title it "Chat Room Evaluation." Save the file as Project 7-1 XXXX 9999, where XXXX is your student ID number and 9999 is your class section number. Use the Print option from the File menu to print your document.

■ To submit your assignment as an e-mail attachment, use a word processing program to compose your chat room evaluation. Save the file as Project 7-1 XXXX 9999, where XXXX is your student ID number and 9999 is your class section number. Open your e-mail software and start a new message. Type your instructor's address in the To: box. Click the Subject box, then type Project 7-1, your student ID number, and your class section number. Attach the Project 7-1 file. Click the Send button or perform any additional steps required by your e-mail software to send an e-mail message.

■Project 7-2: Zipping and Unzipping Files

In this project, you will practice compressing multiple files. You will also gain hands-on experience unzipping files. Finally, you will become familiar with using zipped files as e-mail attachments.

Requirements for this project: This assignment requires Microsoft Windows; either Internet Explorer or Netscape Navigator; e-mail software such as Outlook, AOL or Hotmail; and WinZip. You will also need your instructor's e-mail address. If you are planning to complete this project on a lab or business computer, make sure that you have permission to download and install software on that computer.

Project files needed: No supplemental files are needed.

1. Use your browser to find an interesting text file, a music file, and a graphics file. Save these files on your disk as: XXXgraphic, XXXtext, and XXXmusic (where XXX is your last name).

2. Start WinZip.

3. Zip your text, music, and graphics files into a single file called XXXX.zip (where XXXX is your student ID number) and save the file on your disk.

4. Write down the original size of each file and the size of the zipped file.

5. Start your e-mail software.

6. Compose a message to your instructor and send a copy of the message to yourself.

7. For the subject area enter Project 7-2 XXXX 9999, where XXXX is your student ID number and 9999 is your class section number. For the main body of the message, list the sizes of your original files and also indicate the size of your zipped file.

8. Attach the Movie.zip file to the message.

9. Send the message.

10. After a few minutes, check your messages. You should have received your copy.

11. Unzip the attachment.

12. Open each of the files that you unzipped to make sure that they are the same as the originals.

■ ■ ■

■Index

Page references in bold text indicates a reference to a project.

■ ■ ▮